KEVIN COSTNER
A Life on Film

By the same author

Sylvester Stallone: A Life on Film

KEVIN COSTNER

A Life on Film

Adrian Wright

ROBERT HALE · LONDON

ISBN 0 7090 4700 2

Robert Hale Limited
Clerkenwell House
Clerkenwell Green
London EC1R 0HT

Photoset in Palatino by
Derek Doyle & Associates, Mold, Clwyd.
Printed in Great Britain by
St Edmundsbury Press Ltd, Bury St Edmunds, Suffolk.
Bound by Hunter & Foulis Ltd.

Contents

List of Illustrations   6
Acknowledgements   9
Introduction   13

1   Starting with Rumpelstiltskin   19
2   Walking on   28
3   Birdseed   37
4   Pastorale   49
5   Riding Out   60
6   Doing Good   68
7   Houses of Cards   84
8   The Church of Baseball   95
9   Home Run   105
10 A Monopoly on Passion   117
11 Orson Welles with No Belly   127
12 Two Kevins, Two Robins, and a Race to the
    Finish   143
13 A Downside to Fame   151
14 Dealing with Camelot   161

Bibliography   173
Filmography   175
Index   185

Illustrations

Between pages 56 and 57

1   A montage from the early and forgotten Costner movie *Stacy's Knights*
2   A face that was often left on the cutting-room floor
3   *The Mission* was a little gem hidden away in *Amazing Stories*
4   Looking like a leading man in Steven Spielberg's *The Mission*
5   Horsing around on the set of *Silverado*
6   The quartet of *Silverado* heroes wondering whose drink Linda Hunt is keeping back
7   Al Capone's opposition, also known as The Untouchables

Between pages 104 and 105

8   Brian De Palma talking to his leading man during a break in *The Untouchables*
9   The comforts of home, a vital ingredient of so many Costner movies
10 Second-billed David Grant seems content to let his sick brother take the credit
11 Sean Young and Costner in their Sunday best at the beginning of *No Way Out*
12 Those who wanted Costner as a sex symbol had to wait for *No Way Out*

13 Much of *Bull Durham* is incomprehensible to anyone not brought up on baseball
14 As much about a sense of belonging as about baseball

Between pages 152 and 153

15 Hoping that seeing is believing in the magical *Field of Dreams*
16 Costner cradling the dying Madeleine Stowe in *Revenge*
17 Costner, Madeleine Stowe and Anthony Quinn in a memento of *Revenge*
18 The white man carries Stands with a Fist back to her people
19 Costner as a deeply troubled guardian of America's doubts
20 John Dunbar riding out for America

All illustrations courtesy of the British Film Institute

Acknowledgements

The writing of any biography is not possible without the support of many individuals and agencies, and the debt owed to them is great.

My thanks go to the staff of those libraries that have provided invaluable assistance, notably the British Library, Norfolk County Library, the University of East Anglia, Norwich City College, and Phil Wickham of the British Film Institute Library. For their help in tracing photographs, I am also indebted to the staff of the Stills Department of the British Film Institute.

As always, I must thank those who have helped me trace, or supplied me with copies of, elusive films. In a book that sets out to be the first comprehensive overview of Kevin Costner and his work, it was essential that I see all Mr Costner's films. Ultimately, only *Sizzle Beach* slipped through the net. For their assistance in tracing other material I must thank, among others, Alexandra Shulman, David Lennan, Audrey Prosser, and Samantha King of First Independent Films.

I am grateful to the editor of *Time Out* for permission to quote from that journal; to Pan Macmillan for permission to quote from *The Film Yearbook*; to Marion Boyars for permission to quote from Pauline Kael's *Hooked*, and to Barry MacIlheney for permission to quote from *Empire* magazine. I have also quoted other critics, with whom I might agree or disagree, and I acknowledge their contribution.

Michael King has again provided invaluable technical

assistance and support in the preparation of the manuscript. My last debt is to Terry Dunning, who has given practical help, asked awkward questions, criticized and encouraged.

Poringland, 1992

This book is for Brenda,
who always thought I would write one

Introduction

Kevin Costner might have been a businessman.

Or a hunter.

He became an actor, and the actor became one of the biggest America has offered the world.

From a boy, he thrived on adventure. When he was eighteen, he built a canoe and paddled down rivers that opened out into the Pacific. His romance, as a boy, was to go off for a day's shooting on his own, living the life of a one-day trapper. His life style, his empathy with the great outdoor mentality of an old-fashioned America, seemed to be what was required. It met with the approval of his parents, and young Kevin saw his attitudes and values vindicated by classic American heroes like James Stewart.

James Stewart in *How the West Was Won* meant a very great deal to the boy. In later years, some would say he himself had taken on the mantle of middle-road decency once borne by Stewart. And when Kevin was not being compared to James Stewart, there was always Gary Cooper, presumably because Cooper, like Stewart, like Costner, rode horses in movies and brought a lump to the throat about plain, honest folk living plain, honest lives in America, and used lazy, unhassled accents.

Later, when he became the movie star he overnight determined to become, Philip Blinko described Costner as 'a thinking man's Rob Lowe, a bimbo's Robert De Niro'.

Kevin Costner is the actor who came from nowhere. He is certainly not in the classical tradition, having had none of the stage training that many leading film actors have as their backbone – and therefore he clearly does not subscribe to anything like a method of acting.

Listening to him talking about his craft, it's difficult to know what he does subscribe to, for Costner is not the most eloquent conversationalist. The puzzle behind so many of his statements about his life and films is their lack of clarity, despite the fact that he always seems to be trying to say something meaningful. But actors do not have to be witty or profound in their real lives. And there is always someone offering an overview of his character that confirms what we, his audience, feel Costner is.

For an old friend, director Kevin Reynolds, Costner was 'a throwback to the rogue anti-hero characters of the sixties, yet he's his own man – charming but self-confident, even dangerous. He's a real down-to-earth guy, not at all a Hollywood type'.

It was an opinion Reynolds might have revised after directing Costner in a movie about a man so kind and selfless that he is today remembered for taking from the rich and giving to the poor. If Costner realized there was a real-life difference between true friendship and the exigencies of the movie business, he took no notice of it now.

But, on the sidelines, was always the evidence about what Costner was really like. His pleasures sometimes bordered on the charmingly naïve. He was aged twenty-eight before a smart limousine came to pick him up at his house, but derived as much pleasure from his neighbours, who came out to watch his great moment, this chauffeured acceptance that he had arrived as an actor. The local boy made good took a snap of the occasion, as if such a thing might never happen again. And perhaps the mere fact that his neighbours could feel so warmly about him, that extras working on his movies testify to his kindness, his effort to make their work more pleasant, speaks volumes about the straightforwardness of the guy.

'He's not interested in art or music or politics or anything,' says a leading movie executive who has worked alongside Costner. 'He's not Al Pacino. There's nothing dark in him. If you were talking about Robert De

Niro, I could give you twenty stories. But Kevin's just a Haimish guy, if there is such a word for a Gentile.'

The sort of Haimish guy who, in the movies, can only be personified by one or two great personalities in any one generation. For most of the golden years of Hollywood, the actor who filled this role was James Stewart, whose work so often pointed up the delights and little sadnesses of everyday, downtown America. For a critical overview of Kevin Costner's abilities, Pauline Kael also turned for comparison to the histories of American life stored in dusty Hollywood cans.

'He's James Stewart,' proclaimed Kael, ' ... and Gary Cooper in their Frank Capra roles....'

This was wonderful praise from the doyenne of American critics, who should have known the real article when she saw it. Unfortunately, Kael rather changed her mind about Kevin Costner's abilities around the time his career hit the jackpot. It seemed as if she felt a little uneasy about his success, an uneasiness shared by others who wrote about his industry. And, sometimes, the tone of the new criticism almost passed judgement on his personal qualities, not on his qualities, or otherwise, as an actor. Not surprisingly, Costner made vague protesting noises back at his critics.

'I'm not a prick, not a nice guy,' he argued. 'I just am.'

Not quite, for Kevin Costner is unique among present-day Hollywood actors in several ways, not least the extraordinary way in which he took control of his career at the first possible opportunity, and has gone on controlling it. With only one major exception in the mainstream films he has made (the misplaced *Revenge*) he seems to have made a conscious attempt – often alarmingly successful – to place himself at the helm of popular American culture.

At first sight, this may not seem enough to set him apart from other screen actors, but Costner is in quite a different mould to most of his peers. His culture has nothing to do with the brutish modernity of Bruce Willis or the body-god brigade led by Schwarzenegger, Stallone, Van Damme, et al. He does not have the lightness or obvious warmth of Mel Gibson. When the wits of cinema, among them Woody Allen and Mel Brooks, have promulgated popular American culture, they have looked at it askew. Not so Costner, for there is nothing wry about his attitude to the culture he is representing on screen.

He has taken himself seriously, again and again finding roles that tub-thump everything that is solid and dependable about the American way of life. He has never tired of letting the public and his co-workers know that he has high standards and means to live and act (and direct) by them, and this has been understood by those seeing his work.

At the time of *JFK*, a movie in which Costner, with much brilliant subtlety, placed another huge brick in his wall of American culture, critics readily admitted that, when it came to the current crop of actors, Costner seemed to be the only one in view with enough integrity to bring it off. Part-actor, part-Hollywood-statesman, Costner has acquired a gravitas denied most of the fellow-actors of his generation, and there are always those willing to give a definitive explanation of his qualities.

For movie executive Tom Pollock 'Kevin fulfils many of the same ideals that Jimmy Stewart or Gary Cooper did for their generation: the little guy against the system, the pure guy vs. evil, the strong man in a time of trouble. It is hard to think of any other leading man in his thirties who can play this variety of roles – action hero, romantic lead and family man.'

That Costner has been seen as a force for Good in his movies can't be denied. Leaving behind the unsatisfactory stuff he made when it was a case of working or staying at home watching others take the money, from *The Big Chill* on, he has stood for the old values, firm beliefs, a sense of America's pride. And while doing all this he has tried to find a sense of balance, of personal happiness, of those priorities that mean more to a man than to a movie star. It's a difficult act to sustain.

In the mid–80s, Kevin Costner was the name that cropped up on video releases of cheaply produced, even sexploitation, movies. He had walked away from one feeble project, *The Gunrunner*, thinking it so poor that it had been left unfinished – only to have it come bouncing

back at him six years later, when anything wearing a
Costner label might sell. A few years on, the movie that he
had conceived, nurtured, directed and starred in – and the
movie nobody had been interested in making – picked up
seven Oscars. Not that its not being liked by the
Hollywood studios was anything new to Costner – they
hadn't liked *Bull Durham* either, or *Field of Dreams*, or *JFK*,
or, it seemed, half the movies Costner's name was
attached to.

Throughout, his sense of proportion has seemed
unassailable. Receiving the accolades of the Academy
Awards for *Dances with Wolves*, Costner told the gathering
that, so far as he was concerned, it wasn't the greatest
night of his life. He baulked at the fence of conventional
Hollywood stardom. Again, his sense of balance seemed
to be keeping him up.

That balance has, since the end of his college days, also
involved his wife and family. Here is a man who says he
cares what his parents think, what his wife thinks, what
his children think. He turns words into deeds by having
them along with him on location as often as he can. Here,
too, the pressures of his overwhelming success at the end
of the 1980s began to tell a different, sadder, story.

According to those who know and work with him,
Costner is a man of values, of tenacious belief in what he is
trying to achieve in his work. The standards are high, and
it's not surprising, looking at the spread of his career, that
as that career moved into its second decade, there was a
backlash of some ill-feeling towards him. Where Costner
had once picked up only glowing notices, strands of
criticism were becoming more apparent. What seemed to
some like an almost religious fervour in his work seemed
almost unctuous to others. Perhaps, in a bad world,
Costner was being too good for his own benefit.

But good is what so much of Costner's career has been
about, just as soon as he could get away from workaday
movies that were little more than stepping-stones. Good
shines out of the image he presents on screen. From the
dawning of good in movies like *Fandango* and *Silverado*
through to *The Untouchables* where his character stares
straight into the camera and informs us he is going to 'do

good', reaching an apotheosis in the remarkable *JFK* – Costner's is a very individual contribution not only to cinema but to the way his country's culture is perceived.

And that – for a guy brought up ordinarily in the backwoods of small-town America – seems inevitable.

1   Starting with Rumpelstiltskin

Although it began ordinarily enough, it was a life that wasted no time in trying to link itself up to legend.

The Costners went back a long way. They claimed to have descended from the Kosters, finding themselves with the same (German) name as none other than General Custer – a tangible connection for someone who grew up wanting to have a grand effect on his fellow-man's perception of his homeland. An inescapable truth is that the Kosters were rooted in the establishment of the old West, that slow and painful development of culture that has somehow been subsumed into modern-day America.

In the second half of the nineteenth century a band of Koster brothers, with names that seem to have sprung up out of Paul Bunyan – Dewey, Blacky, Norville, Ilbert and Orville – grew up strong and fearless, claiming a lineage that had resulted in a cocktail of Irish, German and even Cherokee blood. The Koster destined to be Kevin Costner's grandfather took his wife when she was only fourteen, and may have settled down comfortably in Oklahoma. Another version of the grandfather's life is that his considerable wealth was lost in the Dust Bowl during the Depression, and the one-time fortunate was reduced to working as an Okie, digging ditches wherever, in California, they needed to be dug.

Kevin Costner's father, William, grew up a good Republican, but never showed signs of any particularly rare talent – rather, he was respectable, stolid and dependable. Bill made his career with Southern Californian Edison, after moving from his father's farming territory of Oklahoma, turning his back on a steady, homely lifestyle for a new life that would send him travelling all over California, first as a pole-mounter and later, after promotion, as a supervisor.

There was his wife, Sharon, to consider, and she contributed to the family's income by working for the State Welfare Department. By 1955 there were also their two sons, elder brother Dan and Kevin, born on 18 January 1955 in Compton, a city that had begun as a colony of Methodists in 1867, named after the pioneer settler G.D. Compton, only to have much of its fabric destroyed by the earthquake of 1933.

Unexciting as his home-town may have been, Kevin was as fortunate as could be in his parents, at least so far as everything outside his interest in acting and the theatre went – and, as for Bill, Kevin would later say 'He's my ideal of how a father should direct his son.'

The father-son relationship was always good, with Bill encouraging his son's interest in sport and the glories of the open-air life while resisting any tendency to force things on him. A real affection developed between Bill and his boys; at the end of every working day as Bill returned home, the boys would race to unlace his boots as a prelude to the comforts of the evening. The strong, cosy atmosphere of his upbringing, at a time when a host of other families were not so fortunate, didn't leave Kevin untouched.

'As I've gotten older I've questioned my whole conservative background,' said Costner. 'You could say that I have a playground mentality, meaning I think you should be fair about how you treat people.' Not everyone would be happy about using the childhood playground as an allegory of how life should be lived.

One thing that was noticeably missing for many of his early years, however, was the absolute stability that is the bedrock of family life, as Bill's work moved the family from place to place.

As for anything to do with acting, his first real brush with cinema was at age three when he ran into Walt Disney (a man he would have some reason to be grateful to in the not too distant future) on a visit to Frontierland. At kindergarten, he showed his prankish tendencies by jumping off a roof and breaking a big toe. The physicality of his interests was given another boost when his father presented him with his first (real) gun, a Winchester BB, at the age of five. By the time he was nine, one of Kevin's joys was to take himself into the hills for a day's shooting, accompanied only by his dog, in the hope of bringing back a rabbit or quail for the family table.

This predilection for hunting, one of the strongest expressions of the old West, never left him. If he had not become an actor, Kevin's fondest wish would remain that he had been a trapper working in Alaska or the Pacific Northwest. His love of hunting has never lessened and – in these animal-conscious times – seems to have had little impact on the fondness of his admirers.

It looked as if every perfectly adjusted American boy's dream of reliving the life of a classic frontiersman was being worked through, and then James Stewart came along to add strength to Kevin's conviction. Kevin was only eight when he watched *How the West Was Won* in a movie-house, but the film proved to be much more than an afternoon's pastime: it was an extraordinary experience that was never to leave him. This mammoth account of the opening of the Wild West, stage-managed by three directors (Henry Hathaway, John Ford and George Marshall), told a tale of pioneering that went straight to Kevin's heart. Before long, the boy had such an affinity with the movie that he was able to act it out, word for word, scene by scene, though this familiarity was only of superficial importance – what mattered was what Stewart and the film had left in his mind, and the effect they would have on the life ahead.

His first contact with this movie was so intense that when, many years and much success later, he wanted to see *The Untouchables* at a cinema, he couldn't bear to go into the building because it was the house he had first seen *How the West Was Won* in as a young boy. After absorbing the image Stewart presented on the screen, Kevin was able to return to his games of cowboys and Indians with increased meaning, borrowing ponies from friendly neighbours to help live out the fantasy.

But the process of tying up what was happening on a movie screen with sporting activities did not – how could it? – occur to him, though there seems early in his life to have been something of an emotional dichotomy. Other boys might play a game of baseball and talk about their victories with their friends, but Kevin was just as likely to put down his bat and go home to write a poem about what his feelings were.

'I didn't realize which was more important to me,' he said.

His interests in communal activities reflected the two sides of Kevin's persona with some accuracy. If he wasn't competing against other young people of the neighbour-hood in athletics, he was appearing beside them in amateur musicals at the local church. An ability to take non-arty subjects and make them into something wonderful, living and beautiful, suggested itself. Coming home from singing in the church choir, Kevin might sit down to write one of his verses or make an attempt to weave a book around the letters his brother had written him from Vietnam. These meant a great deal to him, and he was very conscious of the seriousness of this separation from a brother he dearly loved and respected.

In trying to give these things a different existence through another art form, Kevin was making his first stabs at creativity, but he never envisaged making this happen by becoming an actor – a notion, anyway, that filled Bill with deep suspicion. For Kevin, acting was something beyond, something only other, predestined, people did, but he was subconsciously doing the most important thing any decent actor can do by way of preparing himself – observing everything around him.

Meanwhile, there was another factor: girls. They didn't present any great problems because there were not many of them in Kevin's life. He never had much sympathy with growing-pained kids in college movies who couldn't get their girls into bed, for neither could he. His short stature, slim frame, and his lack of what other, more worldly-wise guys, thought of as experience, held him back. To compensate for his inability to strike up any long-lasting or meaningful relationship with the opposite sex he took to going out with, as he christened them, 'sluts'.

Kevin was happy with 'slut' as a term of endearment for the type of girl he got along well with, for the type of girl who could be picked up and dropped (something like the giggling girls the Groovers would pick up in *Fandango* many years later). Looking back on his college days, he recalled how important these friendships had been to him.

'At college I began to grow at last and even though I stretched to six feet one I was still nervous around girls. I took to picking up women. I felt more comfortable about sex that way. I preferred flirting to serious dating ... I got used to it. You can talk to a slut.'

Meanwhile, schools predominated – many of them, as the family moved around – and expectations had to be met. Between the ninth and twelfth grades he changed school four times, which didn't make it any easier for the boy to make friends, never an easy matter for Kevin. In high school, the problems did not go away; they increased, as he smacked headlong into adolescence. His confidence was not helped by the fact that he was of puny build, standing only five feet two inches tall in his sophomore years.

'That's the time you get your licence, and it was hard for me to drive, hard for me to reach the peddle. Also, it was embarrassing with girls, who were all taller than me. I wanted to play basket-ball, but I was a little guy. I was a late developer.'

In fact, Kevin regarded himself as something of a turtle, not always rich in the worldly knowledge his peers bragged about. During his time in seventh grade he had to listen to one of his friends telling of how he'd 'balled' a girl, but it was two days later when it dawned on Kevin what the boy had meant. The feeling that he was lagging behind in life, and was being kept in the dark about many of its more intimate pleasures, stuck with him, though he made no pretence at being anything other than a 'typical California jock' who enjoyed drinking beer, being physical and taking part in the odd fight.

University might have been expected to alter all this. Kevin enrolled as a marketing major of California State University at Fullerton, and it seemed to the family as if a respectable career in marketing was opening up for him. Other forces, however, were at work, and about to come together to effect major changes in his life, and a major upset to his family's expectations. By his last year at Fullerton, boredom had set in, and, for the first time in his life, Kevin stopped to take a good look at what lay ahead for him.

First, it occurred to him that he might just be interested in becoming an actor. He picked up a newspaper, the *Daily Titan*, and saw an audition call for an amateur production of *Rumpelstiltskin*. Why shouldn't Kevin be a part of it? But the *Rumpelstiltskin* company wouldn't take him. Expecting no encouragement from his parents, he went through an unexpectedly clandestine phase of appearing with little local theatre groups, without the knowledge of Bill and Sharon. In 1974, he got involved with his first movie, *Sizzle Beach*. He tried out for parts with the South Coast Actors Co-Op, and began taking acting lessons alongside fellow-pupil Greg Avellone.

'Kevin was full of self-confidence. If he had any doubts, he kept them to himself. He really felt that if he pursued it long enough the doors would open for him.'

At Fullerton, Kevin passed the time by joining a fraternity, but it was not a profitable period so far as girls were concerned – any attempts at dating were few and far between. In his second year at university, during March 1975, this changed. The girl's name was Cindy Silva, whose colourful claim to fame at this time was that she played Snow White for Disney at Disneyland during the summer vacation, a testament to her almost classically good looks. For Kevin, from sluts to Snow White was some progress.

The couple met at a fraternity party to which Cindy had gone accompanied by her then boyfriend's sister. That night she and Kevin danced five dances together, but Kevin didn't rate his chances with her, perhaps remembering the rather dubious advice his mother had handed out – that he should never consider dating a girl he wouldn't think of marrying.

Cindy, thankfully, was made of stronger stuff than the greenhorn Kevin. One day she happened by the fraternity house with some butter-pecan ice-cream and persuaded Kevin to come out and taste it. The only decent clothing available to him at that moment was a wet suit, but the friendship was struck, and Kevin went on to ask Cindy if she would go to the movies with him – *Funny Girl* seemed an apt choice. On that date, the proud Kevin took Cindy home for his parents' approval, which was readily given. Bill could now look forward to the union of his sloppy, long-haired, wire-rimmed-bespectacled younger son to a girl who appeared to be a re-mould of Shirley Jones.

'There she was,' said Kevin later, 'so decent, so beautiful, with a glow about her. And she had those big, dark eyes. When I met her I knew that I was a bit of a rascal who went with sluts before. And I really thought no decent woman would have me.'

It was natural that marriage would follow, and, as well as being the prelude to a happy life with Cindy, marriage gave Kevin the spark to light his other ambitions. The couple became Mr and Mrs Costner in 1978, when Kevin was twenty-three.

One important step was taken during the flight back home from the newly-wed's honeymoon in Puerto Vallarta, where one of their fellow-travellers was an actor called Richard Burton. Kevin's off-the-cuff conversation with Burton was something of a milestone in his life, for Burton managed to convince the searching Costner that acting was indeed a great, valuable, life-enhancing vocation and occupation. Kevin seemed to need Burton to tell him that yes, a person could be a good person and an actor at one and the same time, though it is not quite clear who needed such an affirmation – Kevin himself, or those around him.

Burton also pointed out that he and Kevin had eyes of the same colour; according to Burton, Costner's blue-grey eyes could confidently look out at the future.

'What I liked about him,' said Costner, 'was that he didn't say how hard it would be and he never said the obvious things that one must know inherently.'

If Burton's testimony was indeed the final prising open of the gate of Kevin's ambition, it does not seem to have been a very momentous event. Fires were lit in Kevin's mind that would not easily be extinguished, but the pressures of other people's expectations (and, to some extent, of his own) still nagged at him.

So it was that, after arriving home, Kevin put himself through a gloriously brief purgatory of thirty days in which he did at least make some effort to exercise his talents for marketing, but he was completely frustrated by it. The bitterness that he felt, containing the ideas he had about a different life, unable to discuss them with anyone else – after all, who could possibly understand them, or take them seriously? – couldn't be endured.

He told Cindy, in a manner that didn't seem to expect to be challenged, that he was going to be an actor. Whereas Snow White might have merely blinked her doe-like eyes, Cindy flipped. What did he mean, he was going to throw up his career and become an actor? Who wanted him to be one? So far as she could see, her husband was only a little way from being illiterate. How did he expect them to survive, or to make a go of their marriage?

It was immediately obvious to Kevin that producers were not going to beat a path to his door – and while he was beating a path to theirs he had a relationship to work at and sustain. Jobs followed fast on one another's heels. The opportunity to write the screenplays he wanted to create didn't come his way, but there was always some sort of casual labour he could turn his hand to. He would work as a cook on a fishing-smack while taking acting lessons from reputable teachers. Sometimes it was difficult to tell if he was doing a travelling job or had made a profession of bumming around the country. Casting directors turned a disapproving eye on him. One of them was brave enough to explain he simply wasn't handsome enough. Her verdict affected him.

'I never thought I was sexy,' he said, 'and I don't believe it now. What that casting director said to me was hurtful. She was an ass to say it, but I would have been an ass to believe it.'

If there seemed no prospect of working on stage or in front of the cameras, he could at least work behind them, in no matter how humble a capacity, and it was at the Raleigh Studios in Hollywood that he was taken on as a stage-manager. He reasoned that if he was going to take out trash it might as well be movie trash. There were times working at Raleigh when his lowly position had him climbing the walls with frustration.

'I'd walk out of their offices with my fingers in my ears so I wouldn't have to hear someone who didn't know as much as I did telling me what to do.'

Unknown to him, his job at Raleigh Studios set off another of his life's ironies, for he would end up owning the premises and running his own film empire from it. For the present, however, career developments didn't come with startling speed, and Kevin and Cindy had to stand by and watch other contemporary hopefuls getting well ahead of them.

'When they asked me what I was doing, the answer would usually be, "I've got an interview next month" – an interview that the guy might not even show up for. They would look at that, not understand it, and maybe even say something rude. And the ride home would be a very silent one.'

It must have occurred to Cindy that to be an actor the one thing you need to do is act, and the roles simply did not come Kevin's way. So much, anyway, was true of the seventies, except for an early career blip, with Kevin Costner the star of what he looked on as nothing more than a 'tits 'n' ass' movie. At the very end of the decade, however, Kevin's career – very modestly at first – began to move.

2 Walking On

Even when Kevin's movie profile was beginning to look up, there was usually bad news with the good. The good news at this point of his career was that, before long, he was being picked up for small roles by creditable directors, some of whom would go on to use him again later in his life, but for a time it looked as if Kevin's one claim to fame was to be the actor whose screen time was left on the cutting-room floor. As if to aggravate the situation, those movies in which he did manage to survive the editor's scissors belonged to a less reputable, almost twilight, world – the world of exploitation and sexploitation, bordering on 'blue' movies.

Sizzle Beach (sometimes known as *Sizzle Beach USA* or *Malibu Hot Summer*) was made as early as 1974, though it doesn't seem to have been issued in any real sense until the mid-eighties, by which time Kevin's career was well on the way, making its release an experience he would much rather have forgotten. The movie world had its own revenge on Kevin for getting involved in this particular movie; he didn't make another one for the next six years. Produced by Eric Louzil, *Sizzle Beach* was made under the umbrella of the New York-based Troma company which had enriched the movie world with such irresistible offerings as *Rabid Grannies* and *Surf Nazis Must Die*. Whatever else, Troma deserved a prize for juicy, fun titles.

The plot of *Sizzle Beach* had Kevin as a well-to-do young stable-owner John Logan, living in delicious harmony with three scantily-dressed starlets at a house near

Malibu. Landing the contract, Kevin must have thought he had arrived as an actor, but he was much later to look back on the project with very different feelings.

'I thought I had reached the big time with a big role in that movie,' he said. 'We shot it over weekends and it took nearly a year and I had no idea what the finished film was going to be like. It turned out to be a basic tits 'n' ass thing, but what did I know? I was totally naïve back then.'

Certainly, Kevin didn't take the opportunity to argue artistic niceties with *Sizzle Beach*'s director, Richard Brander, who doubled as Kevin's drama coach and fellow-worker at Raleigh Studios. What was more, Brander's wife, Leslie Brander, was starring opposite Kevin, and this made Kevin something of an outsider on the film set, as well as a novice.

'My scenes were with Leslie Brander so I had absolutely zero conception of what was really going on. But the experience helped me. I suddenly knew what type of actor I really wanted to be, and acting became holy to me.'

Such sensitivity didn't prevent the movie resurfacing with regularity in the years to come, with Kevin's increasingly box-office-worthy name used to pull audiences in to see it, but Kevin distanced himself from this young man's folly. He had at least learned a valuable lesson from *Sizzle Beach*, 'not so much because of its low budget, but because of the low budget thinking of the guys who made it. That has stayed with me ever since. These days even on a big budget movie I'm not going to tolerate low-budget thinking.'

But the years had to be filled somehow. Other hopeful young actors might have spent them on the usual circuit of agencies, constantly trying to interest people in a new face, a new image, a new talent. For Costner, this wasn't the way – he looked on acting as something like a religion. He was upheld by the staunchest belief that, along the line, something good would happen to his life.

Cindy, of course, happened, becoming Mrs Costner and, no doubt, looking forward to a successful, regular and somewhat humdrum existence with her new husband. She had every confidence that he would make a success of marketing, while he felt her job with Delta Air

Lines opened the doors for her to climb as high as possible with the company. Cindy looked forward to a married life of dependable ordinariness, supported by a husband who had up to this time seen himself as 'a pattern person, glad to fit in, happy to be somewhere that felt permanent'.

If it was a case of earning money, Costner wasn't work-shy. He framed houses or laboured as need and opportunity arose. When desperation threatened, there was always modelling. Posing for a Gianfranco Ferre tuxedo advertisement kept the wolf from the door for a while. Throughout, he had the support of his own convictions and friends.

'I'm very dependent on my friends,' he claimed. 'And I'm very protective of them. You can't change my mind on people and projects I think are good. Things don't fall out of fashion for me. That could be interpreted as independence – I call it loyalty.'

Two guys who teamed up for friendship with Costner during this time would almost certainly agree with that. They seemed to make a perfect combination, coming together at the beginning of their careers, all of which (thanks in no small way to Costner) were headed for distinction. Jimmy Wilson wanted to direct, Michael Blake wanted to write, and Kevin Costner wanted to act. It wasn't surprising that they decided to start a theatre group between them, developing into the American Twist company that eventually put together their first movie *Stacy's Knights*. This wasn't the movie that would signal an end to Costner's prolonged absence from the screen, however.

Kevin's second effort in films didn't, in truth, show much advance on the first, but it was at least another chance for the novice actor to play a featured role in a movie that made a vague attempt at being professional – the tantalizingly titled *Shadows Run Black*, completed in 1981 but only released two years later. (This fate of having his films held back seems to have attached itself to Kevin's career. *The Gunrunner*, completed in the same year *Shadows Run Black* was finally distributed, only saw the light of day six years later, when the public was at last able to understand why its producers had been shy about exposing it.)

Meanwhile, if the young Costner looked to his co-stars

for inspiration, he must have looked in vain during the shooting of *Shadows Run Black,* whose leading players, the impregnably dull William J. Kulzer and the unprepossessing Elizabeth Trosper, proved a severe handicap. In this company, Kevin already looked about ready to step up and take an Oscar, for he was the only actor in the sorry movie who looked as if he believed the screenwriter's concoction. Basically, this is a tacky story about a serial killer murdering nubile college girls, forever casting off their bras and panties.

Interrupting the tedious soft porn moments, the tale of wizard police chief Rydell King's (Kulzer) investigation into these co-ed killings by the 'Black Angel' unfolds. The first body has hardly been wheeled away before King ('a legend' according to his associates, who has survived the kidnapping and subsequent death of his daughter) is trying to pin her murder on her callow boyfriend Jimmy Scott (Costner). Hairy-chested, short-haired, necklaced, and sporting a fetching blue satin blouson, Scott comes over strongly as a happy-go-lucky young guy with an underpronounced sense of social responsibility. When Lee Faulkner (Terry Congie) is drowned in her pool, Scott is suspected of her murder.

Soon, the killer is moving on to Judy Cole (Trosper), breathing threatening telephone messages to her. And so the plot trundles on until, in a ludicrous finale, King is revealed (long after we have come to our own conclusions) as the Black Angel, acting as a police vigilante to avenge the death of his daughter. He is also obviously a fruitcake, and about to meet his own end by falling from a high roof. We are not allowed this, however, until we have sat through a seemingly interminable sequence of close-up magic, a silly detour into lesbianism, and an encounter with a deranged priest (a so-called 'guest appearance' from George J. Engelson) who claims to have strangled the girls (with his own bare hands which he has named Jack and Bob) – a confession happily snapped up by the wicked Rydell King.

Ridiculous stuff that *Shadows Run Black* so obviously is, Kevin's contribution is the only one of any quality. He gives a real acting performance, with flashes of intuitive feeling, especially in the police interrogation scene where he comes up with mannerisms that would repeat in his later movies. In fact, he seems so involved in the reality of the situation that even the hapless Kulzer comes to life for a few minutes when faced with him, but this is overall a film made by people with no idea of film-making, with the added disadvantage that its one decent actor vanishes halfway through the proceedings.

Presently available prints of *Shadows Run Black* are curious in that all mention of Kevin Costner has been removed from them, presumably at his own insistence. This points to a certain humourlessness about Costner, and a suspicion that he may just be taking himself a little too seriously. Youthful errors of judgement can be an amusing part of an actor's career, and are certainly of interest to the serious moviegoer. Sylvester Stallone did not insist on his name being removed from an early movie of his, very much on the same level of excellence as *Shadows Run Black, No Place to Hide*, and it seems a little petty of Costner to have disassociated himself from the follies of his apprenticeship. This, however, is something he seems to have got into the habit of, distancing himself from several other movies he has made over the years, among them *The Gunrunner, Sizzle Beach* and *Chasing Dreams*. But who wouldn't want to forget such clinkers?

Chasing Dreams was the home-made effort Kevin got himself into in 1981, this one the brainchild of David G. Brown, who wrote, produced and took the leading role of Gavin, a dim young personality who has a younger paraplegic brother and a quarrelsome father. Salvation arrives for Gavin in the shape of a baseball bat when he discovers he's a natural at the game, and he soon has girls and talent scouts vying for his company. Sourpuss Dad ruins it all, and guilt buries Gavin when his brother dies, leading to Gavin's complete breakdown. The happy life is restored when Gavin becomes himself again as soon as his baseball bat is in his hand.

There was nothing to take away the amateurism that went into *Chasing Dreams* – not even Kevin's name some way down the credits. Not to be outdone, the film's makers decided in 1989 that this was a Kevin Costner film, pushing it on to the market with Hollywood's newest star as its selling-point and, apparently, its leading man. Kevin's reaction was to begin legal proceedings against the distributors. But even as *Chasing Dreams* was forced upon a reluctant public, Costner was about to get involved in yet another picture he would have preferred to remain unseen – this time around with Madonna as the undoubted star of the thing.

If catchpenny producers were trading on Kevin's now appealing and good-looking body, he wasn't averse to exploiting these qualities himself, and tried to find a niche as a model. The image that emerged from the photographs coming out of the studio sessions appalled him. They had tried to glamorize him, to turn him into some sort of sophisticate in a desperate attempt to match him up with the product that needed pushing. It made him look, he thought, like a highly-polished assassin, and he didn't want to know. Modelling was thrown over. He must, anyway, have known that his future, uncertain as it might seem, was in the movies, and not to be found hanging around on the fringes of showbiz. He was encouraged in that belief by people in the industry making a note of his name.

An audition for the 1981 movie *Mike's Murder* hadn't proved successful, but casting director Wally Nicita recognized a quality in the young actor that made her take notice.

'He came into my office and did a cold reading for me,' she remembers. 'I explained what the movie was about, what his character was about, and he went outside and took five minutes. He came back and read, and he was fantastic. And I couldn't believe my good fortune in finding someone who was naturally as talented and charismatic. He's so good it makes it look easy.'

Despite her enthusiasm, Nicita didn't cast Kevin for the movie, but pointed him towards Lawrence Kasdan who was preparing a film about a group of baby-boomers reassessing themselves in their maturity. It was a career move that would be of great significance to Kevin.

Fame was proving a curious and unpredictable beast. When, at the end of 1981, Kevin was asked to pose for the cover of the smart up-market magazine *GQ*, it must have seemed like a sort of tribute, even if the fee was a mere $75. At the last moment, the magazine thought better of it, and went for the more mature handsomeness of Zubin Mehta.

Still, the film world had not quite turned its back on Kevin and, through Jane Jenkins, casting director at the Zeotrope Studios, he was listed as a possible extra for any suitable project that might come up.

'Somebody called,' said Jenkins, 'and told me about this guy who was really nice and good-looking and said we should use him as an extra or something. Kevin came over and he was a big, tall guy who was good-looking and smart. So we put him in *Frances*.'

Frances was a biography of the stage and screen actress Frances Farmer, whose heyday in thirties Hollywood had actually produced no particularly memorable films – nevertheless she had been granted an almost legendary status in movie history.

In a list of forgotten films, only *Come and Get It* (1936) – where she played a juicy dual role for Howard Hawks and William Wyler, who said of his star that 'the nicest thing I can say about Frances Farmer is that she is unbearable' – stands out from the dross. Before Hollywood, it had looked as though there was a substantial stage career stretching ahead of her, enhanced by her association with New York's leftish Group Theatre, and her even closer association with its ideological playwright Clifford Odets, but the movies beckoned.

By 1942, worn down by drink problems, husband problems, lover problems, brushes with the police and her efforts to cope with a thoroughly disturbed and overbearing mother, she was playing second fiddle to Gene Tierney in *Son of Fury*, after which Hollywood suddenly didn't call her number any more. What followed was a ghastly seven-year period of incarceration in mental institutions, succumbing ever more to her terrifying mother. Happily, Farmer did eventually emerge into the daylight, writing a painful autobiography and finding a new career as a TV personality in the fifties. Throat cancer killed her in 1970.

The screenplay of *Frances* made much of the most depressing events in Farmer's life, but at least director Graeme Clifford had Jessica Lange making a starry burst at bringing the movie off. Her performance didn't succeed in explaining why the misused Farmer behaved as she did, but this was largely the fault of the script, which wallowed in the later madhouse sequences. Hollywood doesn't appear to have helped Farmer ('I don't know who she fucked to get where she is, but it wasn't me,' says a typically caring studio boss) but, if we can believe this account, she simply handed herself over to the doctors and psychiatrists who set about poisoning her body and mind, ultimately carrying out the horror of a lobotomy. 'Lobotomy gets them home,' chirps the alarmingly confident doctor about to plunge his needle into Farmer's brain.

What we are shown is so horrific and Bedlam-like, with the playing of the mental home's staff so broad, that the movie simply falls apart as it progresses, but it remains a valuable film, for which both Lange and Kim Stanley were nominated for Academy Awards.

Stanley, playing Farmer's mother, probably sent from hell, marked her first appearance on film in fifteen years, and gave a marvellous essay of a deeply troubled woman – alone worth seeking out the movie. This sort of claustrophobic unhappiness had also been expertly conveyed by Stanley in Bryan Forbes' 1964 *Seance on a Wet Afternoon*, playing an unhinged medium persuading her weak husband (Richard Attenborough) to kidnap a child; she had been Academy nominated for this role too.

Costner's role of Luther Adler, a member of Farmer's Broadway company, seems to have suffered during editing, and some reliable sources maintain he was totally removed from the final cut, but he can clearly be seen in two brief scenes, leaving the stage-door with Jessica Lange, signing autographs, taking a peck on the cheek from his co-star, and wishing her 'Goodnight, Frances'.

During the shoot, Costner had protested he wasn't too happy about coming out with that line, a complaint that might have cost him his valuable Screen Actors' Guild card, but he had stayed with the project, even though most of his part had hit the cutting-room floor. A frustrated Clifford finally got Costner's line in the can at four o'clock in the morning. An SAG card had, somewhat reluctantly, been pressed into Costner's hand. Sitting by himself in the extras' bus, the headstrong bit-player admits he felt like 'a complete asshole', but still clung to the belief that his character would not have said 'Goodnight, Frances'.

'I knew Henry Fonda wouldn't have said anything,' Costner argued, 'and Paul Newman wouldn't have. Because it didn't mean anything. It wasn't right.'

What audiences got was a glimpse of a straight-up, confident, handsome, all-American, clean-cut guy, who looked as though he could easily have handled some chunkier dialogue.

What director Graeme Clifford would have thought of building up the newcomer's role is not recorded, but the two men did not finish the movie as bosom buddies. Costner's inability to take his money up front and do the line he was being paid for was a pretty good warning of the type of behaviour he would come up with in the years ahead. When he became a star those around him would have to sit up and take notice of what their leading man said, or they would invariably be the ones who suffered the backlash of his displeasure. The fact that Kevin, so early and at so crucial a stage of his new-born career should put everything on the line because he was unhappy about saying 'Goodnight, Frances' can be read two ways – as sheer stubbornness or as a totally justifiable artistic temperament beginning to stand its ground.

Whatever the reason, and despite everybody assuring everybody else he was a regular nice guy, it was pretty obvious even at this stage that Kevin Costner had the steeliness to make it big in Hollywood.

3 Birdseed

Being billed so far down the credits that the audience was out on the street before his name came up on screen may not have seemed like a harbinger of the sort of career Costner was wanting to carve out for himself, but it was work that director Ron Howard put his way when he cast him for a flash of screen-time as a frat boy in the lovable *Night Shift*.

Not that the role was enough for people to sit up and take notice of. *Night Shift* is truly a comedy, and this has never been Costner's strength; he even manages to look a little uncomfortable in the wild party scene in the mortuary (Costner's only scene, and the weakest in the movie). Thankfully, we have dog-faced Henry Winkler, all tidiness, timidity and earmuffs, handing in a glorious leading performance, abetted by Michael Keaton's hyperactive, wide-spaced but entirely vulnerable hell-raiser, working alongside Winkler in the morgue and getting him to agree that Fate has decided they should become pimps and use the premises as their business HQ.

Costner has so far only made one real comedy movie after *Night Shift*, *Fandango* – where he himself had the responsibility of leading the cast in a movie that, like all good comedies, tries to be more than a comedy. In the later movie, Costner can be seen playing his part in the proceedings without giving himself over to comic playing, and it's a performance that benefits from this reluctance to mug. But *Fandango* was still a long way off, and even when it arrived on Costner's doorstep it obviously was not going to be backed by the studio guns that proclaimed the delights of *Night Shift*. It was left to Costner to prove in *Fandango* that in the movie world small can sometimes be quite beautiful, with a film made in friendship among friends.

Meanwhile, he was involved in a movie called *Stacy's Knights* (also known as *Winning Streak*) that, besides offering him the leading role, consolidated friendships that would bear much more profitable fruit in the years to come. The screenplay for *Stacy's Knights* was by Michael Blake, who went on to write both the novel and screenplay for *Dances with Wolves*, while its director, Jim Wilson, became *Wolves'* producer, before which he had also acted as associate producer on *Revenge*. It was Wilson who, having met Blake at the Berkeley Film Institute, set up the production company American Twist for whom *Stacy's Knights* was the debut film. It was also Costner's first really big movie role to come through. He had taken the afternoon off from Raleigh Studios, turned up for an audition and landed the leading part of Will Bonner. It was a role that exercised many of Costner's particular qualities, and handed him the sort of well-written screenplay he wanted to wed himself to.

Stacy Lancaster (Andra Millian) has driven 200 miles from the Jean Dennison Acting School, where she is studying, to Reno, her one intention to play the casinos there. Bespectacled, mousy, uncertain, Stacy tells Jean (Eve Lilith) that she is trying to get her life and personality together. Jean decides to accompany her on her next trip to the casinos, in an effort to help the girl work out her frustrations. Stacy is on a winning streak but throws in the game, much to the disgust of a young prospecting miner Will Bonner (Costner) who catches up with her and tells her 'You never quit on a streak till it ends'.

Stacy insists she wants to be a lawyer, not a gambler, while Jean insists that Stacy needs to work on her 'power', that she needs to make people stop pushing her around. Returning to the tables, Stacy and Jean are watched over benevolently by Will while the slimeball casino manager Shecky Poole (Mike Reynolds) keeps a wary eye on Stacy's mounting winnings. He cheats Stacy out of her lucky run.

On Will's advice, Jean gets Stacy out of the casino where Will tells them that though Stacy has great potential she needs a good system. He offers his expert tuition for 30 per cent of the proceeds, trusting to his guts ('that's exactly what it takes,' he tells Stacy) that Stacy will prove to be something quite out of the ordinary. Jean goes along with Will's plan, encouraging her pupil.

To teach Stacy everything he knows about cards, Will takes the two women to his uncle's run-down summer cabin. 'This place has everything we need,' he informs them.

'Has it got a broom?' asks Jean.

Will drops the hint to Stacy that Jean looks sloppy and needs to pass as a high-roller if she isn't to attract the wrong kind of attention from the casino managements – Stacy promises to do what she can to change Jean's image. The friendship of the three deepens. Will tells Jean that Stacy looks sloppy and needs to pass for a high-roller if she isn't to attract the wrong kind of attention from the casino managements – Jean promises to do what she can to change Stacy's image.

The girls come back from a shopping spree with smart clothes and sharper looks (Stacy has even ordered contact lenses), and so begins a week of intensive training. They work and play hard. Under Will's tutelage Stacy and Jean make rapid strides until he finally tells them they are ready to hit the casinos ('Anywhere you calculators want to go!').

They go out to a party. Later, alone at the cabin, Will and Stacy fall into each other's arms. When Stacy – known to the casino security men as 'The Mouse' – unleashes her new confidence on the tables and begins cleaning up at Shecky's expense, the casino boss offers the three gambling terrors an all-expenses-paid trip to Los Angeles in his private jet to play at the casinos there. During this visit the management plan to get back the $24,000 Stacy has already won from them.

The gamblers are thrilled to reach L.A., but the casino bosses are far less enthusiastic, being unable to understand how Stacy continues to work her success. They try to wipe her out by cheating her. Now, the situation begins to turn uglier – Stacy, Jean and Will are thrown out and put in the house black book. It seems to Stacy as if everything is over, and she goes out to buy a stack of law-books, much to the annoyance of Will who feels the women have walked out on him. They visit him at the mine, telling him they have decided to call it a day and go back home. Will storms at them for talking 'bullshit'; they haven't got what they came for, and there is still one more card they can play.

Stacy and Jean agree to go with it, and Will takes Stacy to see a guru of the cards, Mr C (Garth Howard), with whom the casinos have long ago come to an understanding – they pay him to keep away from them. Mr C is reluctant to take Stacy under his wing, even though Will explains to him that she is 'as good as Dad was'. Mr C reminds Will that it was gambling that ruined his father.

But Mr C is impressed by Stacy, who reveals herself as a magical pupil. He teaches her how to recognize the life in the cards, drawing from her an almost mystical understanding.

'I've been waiting for you to come along for years,' he tells her as he waves goodbye. 'I never thought you would. Be wise, be careful.'

Stacy, Will and Jean make a determined burst on the casino which Shecky knows has to be stopped when Stacy's winnings overtake £30,000. Shecky accuses Stacy of cheating, but Will stands up to him, telling him she doesn't have to cheat to keep on winning. Shecky has the three of them thrown out and bans them from ever returning.

Cooling off from their adventure, the three relax by the river. Will goes to fish upstream and is set upon by Shecky's thugs. Stacy discovers his body floating face down in the water. When she and Jean try to get a murder investigation under way lawyers maintain it would be a total waste of time, and that they should accept the verdict of accidental drowning. This, of course, is not enough for the newly confident Stacy.

'Will took us both a long way,' she tells Jean, 'but he couldn't take us far enough. We've got to do it. Without him.'

Now, she plans her revenge on the casinos, assembling a new team of counters and going back in for one last enormous win. A male, moustachioed, dapper little Stacy gets back in and cleans up at the tables while a lustily turned-out Jean transforms herself into a steaming vamp charged with the job of keeping the greasy Shecky away from the gambling action. A very great deal of money has already gone when the security men wake up to the fact of Stacy's disguise, recognizing her as the laughable, repressed little 'mouse'. Jubilantly, Stacy, Jean and their gang make their getaway, the richer by $611,000.

'Birdseed,' smiles Stacy.

Stacy's Knights may not have been made on a mega-budget, was not bristling with stars or souped up by brilliant photography and clever post-production, but it was a good little movie that seemed to slip through the net at the time of its issue (not being promoted by the big Hollywood guns was a kiss of death) and has subsequently been mostly forgotten or ignored. But it is interesting for several reasons.

On its own terms, it takes us on a fascinating journey as plain-Jane Stacy, looking remarkably often like a prototype for Dustin Hoffman's Tootsie, learns to unleash her strange powers on unsuspecting crooks running gambling joints, in the process of which her submerged personality breaks through. Top-billed Andra Millian gives a performance that is all the better for not being in the least bit starry; she is always in context, and does wonders with a script that doesn't serve her particularly well. Costner, in what is really his first leading role in a decent film, is totally convincing as he makes Stacy (and Jean, a generous piece of acting by Eve Lilith) unlock the twin mysteries of her strange power and her body.

Throughout, *Stacy's Knights* may be a picture obviously made by youngsters at the movie game, but it pulls itself by sheer skill out of the low-budget, fringe category rut it could so easily have dropped into. Blake's screenplay keeps the watcher's interest while never satisfactorily explaining just what it is that Stacy has, what makes her unbeatable at the tables. Is this a skill she possesses, or a mystical affinity with what is happening to a game? And, of course, Blake is right not to explain any of this; his unwillingness to do so takes the movie from being one-dimensional to existential, for there are many layers at work here.

The very title of the movie suggests a legendary picture of armour-clad male sexuality able to either violate or save maidenhood. Also, the games of the roulette-wheel and card-tables are here cleverly pitched against the more physical games that Jean, Will and Stacy play – snowballing, fooling around with horses. For most of the movie Jean also plays a conniving, utterly amiable and sympathetic role in the growing romance between Will and Stacy.

Through Blake's artful screenplay and the knowing charm of Lilith's performance, Jean becomes part of the trio of sexuality from which she is not spiritually excluded even when Stacy and Will finally get to make love. This game element is also beautifully extended in Jean's final assumption of her Theda Bara-like vamp, having huge fun overstretching Shecky's misreading of female sexuality, at the same time as letting Stacy get away with the haul of her life. By the end of the film, Stacy and Jean have accepted that games, to them, may mean everything; it is Will's most precious legacy to them that no shred of sentimentality about his own loss will prevent them winning, and winning again.

Jim Wilson's able direction of *Stacy's Knights* allowed Costner to work alongside first-rate actors in a movie that had a wealth of warmth and easy humour. Compared with the money he had been commanding, the $500 a week paid to Costner during the shoot also helped him begin to feel like a professional actor. Another by-product of *Stacy's Knights* was that it allowed Wilson and Costner to get to know each other better. Nine years later that friendship would result in Wilson playing his own role as a vital associate to Costner's career, by which time Wilson was in no doubt about his friend's prowess.

'Kevin's an enormous force in the industry,' he asserted. 'Kevin doesn't live by the rules. If there's a rule to be broken, he likes to take that tack. He understands the clout he has, and he's going to use it. He's not sitting back on his laurels saying, "Gee, look how lucky I am – look where I came from".'

From the leading-man status of *Stacy's Knights* it was back to extra work in the mainstream movie world, but at least an extra glorified with the role title of 'Newly-wed Husband' in Robert Lieberman's *Table for Five*.

One of several vehicles for Jon Voight that did nothing to help his standing at the box-office, this was the story of charming but luckless J.P. Tanner (Voight), divorced from his wife who has since married a wealthy lawyer husband (Richard Crenna), and estranged from his three children. As a treat, Tanner takes the children on a cruise, where the four of them (sitting at a table for five that father has, significantly, requested) realize the difficulties of their relationships, and try to come to terms with them. Meanwhile, back home, the children's mother is killed in a car accident, leading the wide-eyed Tanner to realize, after interminable heart-searching, he must get his children back from their new father. Despite a good turn by Voight, the film couldn't sort itself out, suffered from a boring contribution from Crenna, cutesy posing from the children, a sad lack of quality in its leading ladies, and a terminally boring indecision as it meandered to its inconclusion.

Costner's role, strung out over several scenes on board ship, only required him to repeatedly snuggle up to his girl. There was no opportunity to project anything here except an attentiveness to his partner that bordered on the embarrassing. For Sheila Johnston in *Time Out*, *Table for Five* was 'essentially soap opera with fancy production values and grandiose pretensions; the result is the purest kitsch'.

Wally Nicita's thumbs down on Costner when he had tried for the movie *Mike's Murder* was at last paying dividends, for she had passed him to director Lawrence Kasdan who decided to take him up for the movie that would be his own directing debut. By the time *The Big Chill* came along, Kevin had at least fulfilled his life's dream – he was working in pictures – but the pattern that was emerging was hardly the one he had hoped for. Perhaps there were several different patterns emerging.

He had played sizeable roles, and acquitted himself well, in small-time movies that didn't stand a dog's chance of hitting the main movie-houses (*Sizzle Beach, Stacy's Knights, Chasing Dreams, Shadows Run Black*) and had worked himself in at the fringe of mainstream movies as nothing more than an extra (*Frances, Night Shift, Table for Five*). In the small-time films his good work sometimes happened alongside company no decent actor would be seen dead with. In the mainstream movies, it must have been galling to Costner to play chorus-boy while others took the meaty roles and the kudos. Now, Lawrence Kasdan was prepared to alter the balance by offering him a leading role, with other excellent young actors, in a mainstream work. Costner knew he had taken a leap.

'I actually realized it the day I was hired for *The Big Chill*,' he said. 'I felt that a wheel was in place, a very strong one.'

The only obvious down-side to Costner's acceptance of the part was that he had also just been offered the lead in a John Badham-directed movie, *WarGames* – but Badham would have to postpone his chance of working with Costner. No matter. What Costner landed up with in *The Big Chill* was the pivotal (though not the biggest) role, providing the *deus ex machina* of the piece, and the chance to act with peers he could respect, several of whom were also heading for starry careers in cinema: Tom Berenger, Glenn Close, William Hurt and Jeff Goldblum among them.

Costner knew that here he had crossed the threshold of real success. He plunged into a month's rehearsal with the company, followed by the week it took to shoot his scenes. Looking over his shoulder at his past record, he acknowledged that he had all too often in the past been the victim of a cutting-room massacre. He also realized, even as he took the floor, that the very nature of his role in *The Big Chill* meant it was possible for the same scenario to play out all over again.

Costner did his work, took the money, and went home happy. What he didn't know was that when Kasdan looked at the spread of material he had accumulated at the end of the shoot, it was obvious that Costner's character could be dispensed with. This new achievement of being cut out of a mainstream movie indisputably enhanced his reputation as the actor who could be relied on to get himself cut out of any final print. Kasdan personally broke the news to him.

'When the time came and I had to tell him he wasn't in the movie, he reacted amazingly well. I think he was unhappy, but the experience was so valuable to him that it didn't destroy him.'

And there is no doubt that Costner faced the disappointment with equanimity. If there was the slightest suspicion that he had been dropped from the movie simply because he wasn't up to it, this was repudiated by Kasdan's immediate promise to him that they would work together again, and soon. It was a gentleman's promise which Kasdan honoured with *Silverado*. Meanwhile, Costner learned that sometimes the fate of a film must be put before the fate of any individual involved in its making.

'It didn't break my heart to get cut out,' he said. 'I could get cut out of a million movies, but getting cut out of a $100 million hit, that was something.'

'How Much Love, Sex, Fun And Friendship Can A Person Take?' asked the film's advertising, but *The Big Chill* was a much bigger, better and more serious work than the publicity department of Columbia were making out. And it bore the stamp of being about issues that deeply concerned its creator, the writer-director whose *Body Heat* (1981) had shown a masterful evocation of *noir* sexuality, happening for William Hurt and Kathleen Turner. Far away from the sweat and torrid intrigue of this most sensuously pulsating movie, *The Big Chill* seemed to take place on a much more mundane level.

Kasdan and Barbara Benedek's screenplay, recalling a situation that had been played out on similar lines in the 1980 film *Return of the Secaucus Seven*, opened with the funeral of Alex (Costner), the one-time leader of a group of student radicals at the University of Michigan, way back in the simplistically hopeful late sixties. Alex has killed himself, and his erstwhile disciples come to mourn him, but his death is the starting-point of a re-evaluation of their young hopes and aspirations – or what is left of them.

One way or another, every member of the old gang has turned his or her back on the ideals they once clung to. Handsome actor Sam (Berenger) has lowered his sights from a serious attack on the craft of acting to the safety of walking through to fame in a pedestrian TV soap. Meg (Mary Kay Place) had once looked like becoming the female Fiorello La Guardia, a selfless lawyer working on the side of the angels for the world's oppressed against the world's oppressors, but now relaxes in a nicely-paid job for a faceless corporation. Virile Nick (Hurt), whose emotional capacity has been irreparably damaged by the Vietnam War, has found compensation in drugs. Journalist Michael (Goldblum) had set out to be an outspoken exposer of corruption, but has got a living by writing gossipy tit-bits for a scandal magazine.

We can see that Alex has been the first (his prerogative, as leader) of the group to take a hard look at himself. His suicide, presumably, proves he did not much like what he saw. His ability to decide to kill himself is the device that enables his peer group, once under his control, to come together for a mass personal re-evaluation. In death, Alex is thus still very much in control.

For Leslie Halliwell, *The Big Chill* was 'another movie bursting with young talent of the eighties; but none of them became a star in the old sense'. Halliwell's prejudice against anything produced after 1960 is here shown to be a clear case of bad judgement. Danny Peary thought that 'the dialogue is sharp, but too precise (it comes across as if it were written rather than delivered spontaneously)', while Jerome Burne for *Time Out* considered 'the script deftly avoids the twin pitfalls of solemnity or sentimentality which threatens such a scenario; instead, it's perceptive, affectionate and very funny'.

So far as Costner was concerned, *The Big Chill*, even minus his own contribution, was his true arrival in the major league. Three Academy nominations, for Best Actress (Close), Screenplay, and Picture, confirmed its status as a serious work – a long way up from the hole-in-the-corner movies Costner had so often washed up in before.

It didn't matter that Costner was only glimpsed once or twice in the movie. He was keeping good company. His career was lifting off. Two other roles of the period proved this was so – even if one of them was hidden away in the studio's vaults for the next six years.

More fortunate was *Testament*, a made-for-television movie that generated enough interest and praise to earn itself a limited cinema release. An account of the devastating effect nuclear war has on a community in California, *Testament* was made at a time when the fear of such a catastrophe was much more real than it is today. Margery Simkin, when casting the film, had no doubts about hiring Costner.

'Kevin was just sitting in the waiting-room wearing jeans and looking like he hadn't shaved – he looked just like a schlump. But, after he left the room, every woman in that waiting area, and every secretary, came in and said, "Who was that guy?" I've never seen anything quite like it; they just went crazy over him.'

For Lynne Littman, *Testament* was her debut as director, drawing mixed notices for her efforts, but her treatment of a sensitive and frightening subject was thoughtfully worked through, and avoided the overblown techniques of the more block-busting *The Day After*. As the film's star, Jane Alexander won an Academy Award nomination; as a player some way down the credits, Costner wasn't complaining.

'I couldn't play the lead, obviously,' he said, 'because Jane Alexander did, but could I have donned a wig I really would have. I just felt comfortable in being part of something I thought was great.'

Being cast for the lead in a Canadian movie, *The Gunrunner*, may also have looked like a good career move, but this lacklustre piece, directed by Nardo Castillo, was not a happy experience. When shooting wound up, those involved walked away thinking they would never again hear anything of it; so far as they were aware, it had been left unfinished. Not so, if the distributors were to be believed, for in 1989 it was pushed on to the video market on the tide of the Kevin Costner wave.

Those unfortunate enough to sit through *The Gunrunner*

may be beguiled by its atmospheric opening scene: Costner getting ready for bed and lying, hot, sweating, restless, under his mosquito net, but then there was the small matter of the next eighty minutes spent waiting for the film to begin.

Ostensibly, it is about Costner's gunrunner Ted Beaubien's adventures in China and Montreal during the mid-twenties. He has come home to Canada from China, where he supplied weapons to the struggling people. ('They believe in a new China, run by Chinese' is only one of the deeply meaningful lines.) His girlfriend had been killed there in the conflict. Back in Montreal ('American plumbing and French morals'), Ted and his brother become involved in gang warfare, blackmail plots and speakeasies, run by the almost ludicrously vampy Maude (Sara Botsford) who soon proves herself a very dangerous animal indeed.

After an unlikely flirtation ('It's difficult to decide whether you're a hunter or a predator') Ted and Maude go to bed together, but are soon locked in a life-and-death struggle of survival of the fittest, as the story ties itself in ever more mystifying knots. Many deaths later, Maude is also killed, leaving Ted to prepare for his next incursion into China – he is still the gunrunner.

This was a movie for those who liked their Costner strong and silent, rather boring, and at any cost. Insufferably dreary, slow and characterless, it couldn't be saved even by Costner's skill. The whole tedious mess looks as if it has been thrown together with scant regard to clarity or plausibility and, with many scenes ending in a fade-out to black, as if it has been made for television. The period atmosphere (such as it is) doesn't help either, including the sequences in Maude's dangerously-underpopulated nightclub, with its crooner extolling the film's presumed message that 'A Man's Got To Do What His Destiny Leads Him To'. Post-production interference is also clear; some lines credited to Costner, either off-screen or when he has his back to the camera, are spoken by a different actor.

If Kevin Costner was not going to regret turning his back on a lucrative business career, he was going to have to do a lot better than this.

4 Pastorale

There are two figures that play crucial roles in the establishment of Costner's unique screen image, both of them directors: Lawrence Kasdan and Kevin Reynolds. To them may be traced the confirmation of Costner's particular talents, and both of them handed Costner second chances to make it good.

It was to Reynolds that Costner's career now turned. That director had once turned down the actor for a leading part in his college movie *Proof*, preferring to cast another young hopeful. Now, properly budgeted and looking to the mainstream cinema houses, Reynolds – further enhanced by having been taken up as a protégé of Steven Spielberg – was remaking *Proof* as a movie called *Fandango*, and this time the door was wide open for Costner to play the leading role. Not that he had it handed to him on a plate; Kevin was merely one in a long line of hopefuls turning up for an audition.

By the time Costner walked into the room to face Reynolds, the director had seen and turned down over 200 actors for the leading role. Within fifteen seconds of Kevin picking up the script Reynolds knew he was home. He had not only found his leading man, but a good friendship that would endure through the years of Kevin's early success, at least up to the time of *Dances with Wolves*.

For the present, *Fandango* would be the first film to truly test Kevin's talent, his technique, his ability to come across as something quite out of the ordinary. Whether the actor realized its significance is not known, but here was a very important milestone in the development of a young actor trying to make it as a serious artist. It was a magical knack of *Fandango* that its life-affirming story was so perfect for Costner at this stage of his career.

In May 1971, graduation week in Austin, Texas, a brat pack of college buddies, The Groovers, celebrates success or failure, and the imminent marriage of Kenneth Waggener (Sam Robards). The wild party, presided over by the leader of the bunch, Gardner Barnes (Costner) and disapproved of by the punctilious little swot of the gang Phil Hicks (Judd Nelson), breaks up when an ashen-faced Waggener announces his marriage is off. He has received his draft papers – Vietnam beckons. Gardner, Phil and the stolid, reliable priest-to-be Dorman (Chuck Bush) have likewise been drafted, and Gardner is jubilant.

'The Groovers are saved,' he cries, and leads his three mates, accompanied by the goofy Lester (Brian Cesak) who remains drunk and insensible throughout the film, out on a farewell fandango.

Exhilarated, they make off for the Mexican border, for Gardner tells them the time has come for them to 'dig up Dom'. Phil, whose car has been commandeered for the madcap escape from the reality of what awaits them back home, locks himself inside with Dorman and won't hear of driving the 400 miles to the border – it's his job to get Waggener back safe and sound for his wedding. Waggener explains that he has already telephoned his girl's father and told him the marriage is off. Dorman lets Waggener and Gardner into the car, overpowering Phil's wish to head back.

As they drive towards Dom, Waggener wants to phone his girl, while Gardner maintains that, so far as he is concerned, he has never in his life been serious about a woman. We immediately see this is untrue, as a flashback shows a lithe, half-naked Costner doing a dance of love through soft-focus photography with a creature who clearly enchants him. More prosaically, Phil's car now runs out of juice in the desert, but conveniently close to a locomotive track. Gardner's first suggestion is that the dare-devilling Groovers jump the train, but his next brain-wave is to hitch the car to the train's rear carriage.

'It'll be just like water skiing,' he promises, opening up one of the film's most hilarious sequences.

Pushed together at this turning-point of their lives, they look ahead with differing feelings. Waggener tells them he is proud to be going to Vietnam, while Phil sees it as his duty and derides Gardner, who wants nothing to do with it.

The boys get the broken-down car to a gas station, where, at a nearby spot, James Dean had shot *Giant* in 1955. Getting food at a drive-in, they meet two giggling bimbos who take them to what they describe as their local dance-place – a wonderfully Gothic cemetery – after the boys have failed to come up with a better idea.

'What d'ya wanna do now?' one of the girls asks.

'Are you eighteen?' asks Gardner.

The girls delight in firing off rockets and fire-crackers around the headstones of the night-black graves, and soon the cemetery is ablaze with a brilliant firework display. In all this fun, Waggener and Gardner fall to the ground and come face to face with the memorial to a 19-year-old soldier killed on the battlefields of Vietnam. They turn to see the graveyard made fantastic by the exploding lights – a beautifully achieved allegory of what they will themselves be facing in the coming months.

'I'm not sure I can do it, Gardner,' admits Waggener. 'I'm not sure I can go.'

'Then don't,' replies Gardner.

When the boys visit the spot where James Dean had set about immortalizing himself, there is nothing there but a derelict skeletal shell of a set – another dream completely erased. It is a significant disappointment in their progress from the innocent beliefs of youth. The past is opened up again as Gardner and his girl play ball together, lovingly, on banks of white sand. But Gardner must cope with the present, and is challenged by the outraged Phil who tells him to face up to the truth that the days of the Groovers are over.

'Nobody cares about epic adventures any more,' says Phil.

'Philip, we came out here to try to forget some things, right? So why won't you let us? There's nothing wrong with goin' nowhere, son; it's a privilege of youth.'

Feelings between the gang boil over, ending in Gardner's blunt statement that none of them has ever even liked Phil, only taking him on and accepting him as a member of the pack because they felt sorry for him. Worse, Phil is a 'weeny', which he loudly denies, serving notice on them that he's willing to prove he isn't, anywhere, any time.

That time is only a few yards ahead down the road, where Phil is driven to a dilapidated parachute jumping school owned by the wide-eyed, space-brained and delightful ageing hippy Truman Sparks (Marvin J. McIntyre) who lives there with his statutory hippy girlfriend.

Telling Truman they are reporters on a special project for the *Milwaukee Daily Moon*, and that they believe the school is sitting on prime development land, they persuade Truman to give Phil a quick course in parachute jumping, followed by a drop. Terrified of heights, the cringing Phil eventually agrees to go through with it to prove his own bravery, but only if Waggener swears he will not dodge the draft and escape to Mexico with Gardner. Waggener swears to it.

The crazily inept tuition having been got through, Phil is taken up by Truman, taking the opportunity to smoke a joint, while below Truman's girl complains that they've packed her washing, thinking it to be Phil's parachute. Appalled that things will go very wrong, the gang try to spell out on the ground warning messages to Phil that he should not jump, but Truman pushes Phil out of the plane and, as he hurtles down, Truman's washing flies up. Truman frantically radios Phil to pull the lever on the emergency parachute ('We're talking mega-malfunction here,' he roars) and Phil manages it at the last moment. The boys are ecstatic, while Gardner promises the brave parachutist he had not meant a word of what he had said. Truman takes a snapshot of the reunited Groovers, and Phil treasures it, can't stop looking at the picture. He tells Gardner they must go ahead and finish what they have come for – they must find Dom and dig him up.

Hidden in the mountains, they find Dom – a bottle of champagne laid down against the maturity of their young manhood – and each takes a swig from him.

'Here's to us,' shouts Gardner from the edge of a high mountain, 'and that, and the privileges of youth. Here's to us, and what we were.'

'And what we'll be,' adds Phil.

'And what we'll be,' agrees Gardner, tossing the bottle into the air.

For Waggener, the time has come to face the stupidity of having turned his back on the girl he wanted to marry. He can't stop thinking of her.

'That's all love is, mostly,' says Gardner, 'thoughts.'

Waggener telephones his proposal to his girl and is accepted. Now, the gang decide on a fairy-tale wedding, bringing the girl to them rather than returning to Dallas for the ceremony. And who else but Truman can be entrusted with fetching and bringing the bride to her young lover? By a brilliant sleight of hand, Gardner persuades the happily compliant locals to help put on a top-notch wedding. Suddenly, wherever Gardner is becomes Frank Capra country, where human beings are magically linked together in a chain of love and caring. Truman, after a typically hair-raising expedition, gets the girl to her groom on time.

We know, of course, that this girl – now to be Waggener's wife – is the girl Gardner once loved. But Dorman marries her to Waggener as Gardner smiles gently on at them, satisfied with how their lives have worked out. Gardner faces the girl and they stare at one another, full of understanding and a new maturity.

'Hey, how about a fandango?' he asks, and they move together into a last dance. All around them, we have a sense not only of pure Oklahoma but of pure *Oklahoma!*, as the movie ends in a blissfully reflective mood, all promises of gingham and soft moonlit nights. Vietnam, for the moment, lies forgotten.

Despite, or perhaps even because of, its topical and contentious theme (to dodge or not to dodge the inflicted conscription) *Fandango* struggled to earn much success at home in the States, was denied a proper cinema release in Britain (although it played on television), and only managed to really find true recognition in Europe, where it was readily welcomed as something of a cult movie.

Critics at the Venice Film Festival applauded it loudly, seeing in Kevin Reynolds' screenplay and direction a very real promise of great movies to come. For Costner, this was probably just as true, and he must have hoped that, years later, Reynolds would make a splendid movie of *Robin Hood: Prince of Thieves*. Clearly, the two films are so different in style, conception and purpose that it isn't very sensible to make comparisons, but it cannot be denied that in every possible respect poor forgotten *Fandango* is a much better movie than Reynolds' *Robin Hood*.

Most of the public, sadly, have been kept in the dark about its pleasures, not always helped by critics whose faint noises have restricted the movie's popularity. Irma Velasco writing in *People* at least praised its star. 'Costner does seem as if he could talk a riled-up ratler (sic) out of his fangs – he has an easy charm and, for a Southern California native, a not-too-affected Texas twang ... *Fandango*'s real problem is that it doesn't know what to be – a love story? an anti-war statement?' Velasco's mean-spirited perception suggests that the movie cannot be pigeon-holed into a convenient and easily understood category, but, if this is true, it is surely one of *Fandango's* most charming qualities.

Fandango has so much to recommend it to the intelligent and feeling cinema-goer – great performances, a good script, knowing direction, and enough set-piece sequences of wit and excitement to reactivate the most world-weary. Looking at the achievements of *Fandango*, some feeling must be spared for its director, of whom one ends up asking 'What happened to all this promise?'

As for Costner, there was now ample proof of his qualities as a screen actor. He was on his way, and feeling comfortable and supported by the agent that would stay with him through the years of his climb to the top – until Costner felt the need to finally give himself over to the big league agents. J.J. Harris always felt that this young client was headed for the stratosphere. And, unlike so many other actors, Costner had a very strong idea of where his career should be going, what his next move should be.

The lead in *Fandango* had been just such a move. Gardner is a role that serves him admirably, and there is the strongest sense that Costner is acting almost as an abbreviation of contemporary American culture, acknowledging that life has a history and future, that crucial to the making of American man is his ability to look back and onward. There is such a strand of understanding of the past in Gardner, who recognizes the importance of the passing of childhood and adolescence, and will not rest until he has somehow cast this light of understanding around those he loves. Costner's is a performance of such strength, wit and poignancy that one wonders why more critics did not pounce on the evident joy of it. For those who take the trouble to seek it out, *Fandango* gives Costner his first substantial opportunity to make a definitive statement of the American myth in a movie that deserves to be reassessed.

Chasing good scripts, Costner eventually caught up with *American Flyers*, a Warner Bros project to be directed by the British-born, Yale-educated John Badham, whose *WarGames* Costner had turned down in preference to *The Big Chill*. As it happened, *American Flyers* turned out to be something of a curate's egg. It owed a deal to the style of movie-making that Sylvester Stallone and John G. Avildsen had made so fashionable with the original *Rocky* (at its core, a human story of struggle and love married to a gruelling sporting challenge that is ultimately, and triumphantly, overcome) and is one of the long line of movies with strong sport themes that Costner has got involved with over the years. Whereas baseball provides the *raison d'être* for *Chasing Dreams, Bull Durham* and *Field of Dreams, American Flyers* covers bicycle-racing, and the attempt by our two heroes to crack the most demanding bike race of all, the Hell of the West. The picture wasn't one of Costner's happier experiences.

One of the brightest things about it was its creator, Steve Tesich, a writer with a heavy personal commitment not only to his craft but also to bike-racing, which had proved an essential component of his screenplay for the vastly successful 1979 *Breaking Away*, directed by Peter Yates. Of Yugoslavian birth, Tesich had emigrated to Indiana when he was an impressionable young teenager, and went on to enter and win the 1962 Little 500 bike race.

His brilliant work for *Breaking Away* is enough to make us realize that something, somewhere along the line, must have happened to his screenplay for *American Flyers*, for it is light years away from the earlier movie in quality, even though both are solidly set in the hinterland of Middle America.

But Costner and Tesich hit it off well on a personal and professional level, even to the extent of getting on bikes and racing each other to a finish in the true spirit of the film. Tesich recognized in Costner a man he could come to like and work with.

'I saw him in a bar once,' he said, 'saw him leaning on the bar, and I've never seen anyone look better leaning on a bar. Men tend to be very guarded with other men. He's not, and I'm not, and that's why we get along so well.'

Costner was altogether less happy about his director, whose own comments about his leading man smacked of frustration, after Costner had persisted in putting forward his own ideas and questioning decisions made around him.

'His mind was working all the time,' said Badham. 'Ninety per cent of the time [his thoughts were] an improvement, but it was almost a relief to get him on the bicycle.'

It was a relief, too, when the movie itself got into the saddle, for out of it *American Flyers* seemed awkward and unfinished, with drama definitely of the melo variety. What the picture tried to take on board, over and above the bike-racing theme, was the difficulties of love – brotherly love, familial love, love between a cool mother and headstrong son, love between an overweening mother and devoted son, puppy love, and, just before the credits roll, all-forgiving love.

David Sommers (David Grant) has been left at home with his mother (Janice Rule) following the death of his father from cerebral aneurysm, from which Mom now suspects David is also suffering. David's too-long-absent, elder, doctor, brother Marcus (Costner) turns up late to a family reunion, tells Mom that David should cut the apron-strings and get to college, and briskly informs her that she made his father's last days of life hell.

A montage from the early and forgotten Costner movie
Stacy's Knights, with Andra Millian as the girl with a rare gift
for winning

A face that was often left on the cutting-room floor, but was beginning to get noticed – as here, in the nuclear holocaust drama *Testament*

Dismissed at its premiere as an unimportant made-for-TV effort, *The Mission* was a little gem hidden away in *Amazing Stories*. Stagey and whimsical, it nevertheless showed that, even in Hollywood, small can be beautiful

Looking like a leading man in Steven Spielberg's *The Mission*

Horsing around on the set of *Silverado*. His sassy portrayal of Jake is one of Costner's most appealing performances, and proved he was no slouch when it came to guns and horses

The quartet of *Silverado*'s heroes (*left to right* Danny Glover, Kevin Kline, Scott Glenn, Costner) wondering whose drink Linda Hunt (watched by director Lawrence Kasdan) is keeping back

Al Capone's opposition, also known as The Untouchables: *left to right* Charles Martin Smith, Costner, Sean Connery and Andy Garcia

'I could be crazy about you, Mom, but I'm not,' he admits.

Meanwhile, in the kitchen, David is having a dizzy spell and yet another headache. Big brother Marcus takes David (and his bike) back to room with him in Madison, at the house which he shares with his live-in girlfriend Sarah (Rae Dawn Chong). David fondly remembers their boyhood. Marcus introduces David to Dr Conrad (John Amos) of the Sports Medicine department of Wisconsin University (roughly translated motto: 'If You've Got It Up, Keep It Up') who puts David through torturing tests of stamina and a cancer scan.

Subsequently, David overhears Marcus and Conrad talking about the results, and assumes his worst fears are true – he has inherited his father's disorder. Marcus tells David his tests were clear (which David perceives as Marcus trying to keep the bad news from him) and goes on to suggest the two of them should enter the Hell of the West. Repairing the damage done by their years apart, they get to know one another anew as they race bikes together in preparation for the big event.

Soon, David is fixed up with a sassy hippy, Becky (Alexandra Paul), but the general air of happiness is threatened by Sarah's ex-husband, the snaky Muzzin (Luca Bercovici), an arch-enemy of Marcus for personal and sporting reasons – Muzzin was the winner of the last Hell of the West. Dirty work is afoot whenever Muzzin is about, but it is pretty obvious – how could it be otherwise? – that one of the Sommers brothers is going to be mounting the winner's podium this time around.

Before too long we can appreciate Tesich's none-too-subtle plot twist – that Marcus, not David, is the sick brother. At least, this seems to be what we are told, but what is the sickness Marcus succumbs to? Is it cerebral aneurysm? Is it a nose-bleed? By the end of the movie, which of course coincides with the end of the bike race, it is David, straining himself to the edge of endurance, who pushes Muzzin out of the lead, not brother Marcus, who can only look on weakly but adoringly. Mom has also got to the finishing line so that her sons can wrap themselves in her arms. Winning the race has supposedly answered all the family's doubts about their love for one another.

There are enough incidental delights (Dr Conrad's slobbish Bunter-like teenage son resisting any attempt at fitness training; two good performances from the two young leading ladies; a great sunny performance from David Grant, and, above all, the excitingly shot racing sequences) to make *American Flyers* enjoyable, but Badham's treatment betrays uncertainty and muddle. The unfortunate mother, for instance (glacially played by Rule) remains an enigma because we never have her unhappy relationship with the husband or elder son explained. Muzzin's villain is also so exaggerated that he seems to belong to another picture, before undergoing a rather mysterious, and unexplained, change of heart.

Ragged moments of obvious improvisation, and the general disorganisation of the story, suggest not only a troubled shoot but a difficult post-production. Anyway, the film's star was not ecstatic about how the movie had turned out.

'I was in love with Tesich's script,' confessed Costner, 'but not with Badham's directing ... I believe your word is your bond. I'll do anything for a director who promises he won't let me look foolish. I'll risk looking foolish knowing he won't let me.'

And Costner went on to point out that 'the makers of *American Flyers* had taken out everything that mattered to the film'; the critics seemed to agree. Roger Ebert thought the movie was 'a bike race surrounded by giant, unanswered questions ... maybe the approach would work if there weren't so many enormous inconsistencies and loose ends and puzzlements'. For David Ansen in *Newsweek* 'the details and dialogue are consistently superior to the sappy themes. So is the quietly powerful Costner'. The picture got disappointing returns, and no release in Britain.

We can only guess at how Costner would have emerged from the movie had it been a more satisfactory experience. For devout admirers who prefer their Kevin Costner with a bristling moustache and cycling-shorts, *American Flyers* is the movie to seek out. More subjectively, it offers a somewhat po-faced Costner, eclipsed by the openness of tight, muscular, snub-nosed co-star Grant. There is a distinct air in *American Flyers* of a Costner beginning to take himself a little too seriously (or, perhaps, playing a character who takes himself a little too seriously) – and this is a Costner who, from this time in his career, seems to crop up quite regularly.

One of the most positive things Costner could take away from *American Flyers* was his friendship with Tesich – a writer that deserves to be linked up with Costner again. It's only a pity that *American Flyers* didn't turn out better for both.

5   Riding Out

A myth is only a myth as long as it can be sustained, and it was here that the other of the two directors crucial to Costner's fate made a reappearance. Lawrence Kasdan had had no doubts about Costner's potential since *The Big Chill*, and Costner had thankfully never been soured by the experience of being cut out of the finished movie. *Silverado*, Kasdan's new project, would make up for this indignity, and – besides being a major, noticed film where it would be almost impossible for even the most negligent to overlook Costner – it was a Western. As such, it proved an essential episode in the star's life and destiny. A few years later his own beloved attempt at a Western would lead to his most lauded success, and the absolute triumph of his ascendancy as a representative of the total American myth.

In 1985, however, Hollywood was no longer having an affair with the Western film, first-division John Wayne down to third-division Guy Madison long ago having been sent riding off into the sunset. Michael Cimino's budget-exhausting attempt to reassert the Western in 1980 with *Heaven's Gate* had unleashed much critical scorn on this three-hours-plus effort, during the making of which, according to some who gloated in its box-office failure, Cimino had behaved with all the restraint of Erich Von Stroheim.

Now, it seemed as if Hollywood would be making certain trouble for itself if it put up the money for another tale of the old West. It was in 1985 that two interesting movies made a bold attempt to reintroduce fables of America's past to movie audiences: Clint Eastwood's *Pale Rider* and Kasdan's *Silverado*. If neither was a completely successful venture, both were fascinating near-misses.

Pale Rider's overriding recommendation was that it was clearly a Clint Eastwood film, with Clint Eastwood directing actor Clint Eastwood in the leading role of a movie aimed at fans of Clint Eastwood. Here, modernity's Dirty Harry became a mysterious horseman – an essential of the traditional Western, bringing good and demanding justice, like Shane or the Lone Ranger – making the West a less wild place for decent folk to settle in. The issues were clear-cut, obvious and understood, as they were in *Silverado*, which was otherwise a much more discursive work.

But Costner felt he was in the right movie with the right director, and would go on to describe his new project as 'a really fine movie. It makes your heart feel good'. Playing the gawky, gun-slinging, hyperactive and loopy younger brother to Scott Glenn would prove another brick in the wall of Costner's image, though his grip on the role didn't always make life easy for those working alongside him, including his director.

'In practically every scene he was opinionated about what he could do,' said Kasdan uncomplainingly. 'He's like a well, always coming up with ideas, but I couldn't listen to ten ideas every time.'

The movie matched Costner with considerable talents. The Magnificent Four conceived by Lawrence and Mark Kasdan's screenplay were headed by Scott Glenn, whose own slowish development as a screen actor proved that Costner did not have to worry about rushing into stardom. Glenn had been twenty-nine when he played his first movie role in 1971, and had only graduated to really substantial parts some ten years later.

Two other interesting actors, both of whom would go on to considerable success, made up the four heroes of *Silverado* – Kevin Kline and Danny Glover. In preparation for the shoot, the quartet flew out four weeks early to the location at Santa Fe, New Mexico, to practice their horse skills. For Costner, it was a dream come true – a leading

part in a major Western. Kasdan had written the role
especially for him. Kevin's enthusiasm was limitless. His
unusual keenness had him turning up on the set even on
the days when he had not been called – not standard
Hollywood behaviour. And so Kasdan unravelled his
complex, meandering tale of the old West.

Two renegade cowboys, Emmett (Glenn) and Paden
(Kline), team up after Paden's horse has been stolen and
he has been left for dead. Travelling on to the next town,
Paden discovers his horse, kills the thief, kisses the horse,
and comes face to face with the bad-looking Cobb (Brian
Dennehy), who wants Paden where he was once before,
in his employ. Paden refuses. In the saloon, a black
cowboy, Mal (Danny Glover) is refused a drink by the
landlord and attacked by roughs, interrupted by the
English Sheriff Langston (John Cleese), who tells Mal to
get out of town. Emmett learns his kid brother Jake
(Costner) is to be hanged next morning for a killing which
he insists was done in self-defence; the jury has decided
otherwise. When Paden kills the man he finds wearing his
hat, he too is put in jail with Jake, but they make their
escape and ride off alongside Emmett. Mal saves them
from Langston's ensuing posse, and the four escapees ride
off into the wide-open country – one of the film's most
heart-stopping moments.

A wagon-train heading for the town of Silverado is in
trouble, for bandits have stolen all the traveller's money –
without it, they have no life in Silverado. Paden, Emmett
and Mal retrieve the hoard, leaving Jake to lead the train
into safe country, and on their return Paden decides to
stay with the train to be with his pretty lady, Hannah
(Rosanna Arquette), whose philosophy is simply
expressed as she looks out at the great expanses of
uncultivated America.

'It's all I've ever wanted. Pretty land, isn't it? ... After a
while I won't be so pretty, but this land will be.'

It is a time of reunion as Emmett and Jake visit their
married sister, and Mal goes home to find his aged father,
now a widower, hiding out in the hills from the murdering
gang of McKendrick (Ray Baker), whose father Emmett
had shot down in self-defence some years before. In

Silverado, Paden enjoys a drink in the saloon presided over by the diminutive Stella (Linda Hunt) and the two form an obvious, immediate liking for one another, despite Paden learning that Stella's boss is none other than Cobb. There is more bad news to come – Cobb is also the sheriff of Silverado.

McKendrick's men kill Mal's father. Cobb kills the gambling manager of his saloon and appoints Paden in his place. Meanwhile, Emmett and Jake look to move on to California, but, at a party at their sister's house, McKendrick's men attack and kidnap her young son. Emmett meets McKendrick, who tells Cobb he wants Emmett got rid of, and Emmett is indeed captured and about to be despatched when again Mal arrives to rescue him. Weak as he is, Emmett is appalled to hear of the boy's kidnap and rides off with Mal – who has himself escaped from prison with the help of his repenting good-time sister Rae (Lynn Whitfield), escaping from the clutches of a no-good professional gambler Slick (Jeff Goldblum). As Emmett and Mal ride off, Paden joins them.

With the help of a stage-managed cattle stampede, they rescue the boy, and the four heroes ride into Silverado for the final confrontation. Slick is killed by Mal (another self-defence killing), while Paden stands against Cobb to once-and-for-all settle the old score between them. It is, of course, Cobb who falls to the ground at the end of this almost *High Noon* sequence. The four saviours of Silverado lift their glasses and drink to California; Jake and Emmett want to leave for it at once. Paden has found his own place, Silverado, and decides to stay for at least two good reasons – because Stella is there and because he has succeeded Cobb as the town's sheriff. Mal hitches a wagon with his sister, and the two ride off to a good brother-and-sister life in some new place. Emmett and Jake blaze off out of town.

'We'll be back,' roars Jake with one last backward look.

Brought in for $26 million, *Silverado* managed to take only $16 million at the box-office ('Let's just say we did our job better than they did theirs at the studio,' complained Costner) with critics lining up to praise or decry it. Pauline Kael came to bury the movie, not to praise it.

'Kasdan is an impersonal craftsman,' she wrote, 'hip in a post-modern way that's devoid of personality. Probably, to enjoy the movie you'd have to watch it as a cool, Western equivalent of TV's *Miami Vice* ... In this arch, uninvolving atmosphere, every time the director shows his good intentions ... the film gets groggy.'

For Philip Bergson, the trouble was that the movie was 'high, wide and long, over-peopled by a mess of confusing characters – enough almost to sustain a series – the grab-bag of Western ingredients that have gone into *Silverado* at least ensure it is an enjoyable, if eccentric, gallop back through Hollywood trails that have lately become rather dusty'. Richard Corliss in *Time* was another to come up with moderate plaudits, listing the up-and-coming cast but noting that 'almost none of them look at home on the range'. He went on to note that in the past '[Kasdan] has performed deft surgery on the Saturday matinee serial and the *film noir* melodrama. But the Western will not yield.'

Costner's opinion of the movie remained much more unequivocal. 'I thought *Silverado* was a really good film,' he said. 'It had a lot of spirit, it was real intelligent, and it was good theatre.'

Certainly, it had four splendid performances from its leading men, with the lion's share of the glory going to Glenn and Kline, while Costner's role is the smallest of the four. What he achieves in this sketchy part is nevertheless quite considerable, painting a glorious picture of a stringy, demonically active late adolescent on the fringes of man-hood (and thus reminiscent of the situations of *Fandango*). When we first see him he is swinging from the bars of his condemned cell, almost blithely having accepted his impending fate on the scaffold. He is all energy, all uncomplicated sappy youth.

This immaturity finds terrific expression, too, in Cost-ner's evident delight in the fancy horse-work he displays on camera, the nifty way he has with a gun. There is a fabulous physicality to it all, convincing us that Costner approaches the part from the viewpoint of much more than a mere actor. Through his portrayal of Jake, Costner is able to go back to the delights of his own upbringing.

'I used to play cowboys and Indians and practise just

how fast I could jump on a horse and get away,' he said. 'I was always very excited about that stuff.'

It is his real achievement that he gives us a character with a minimum of dialogue to help him out – Jake, courtesy of Costner, is more of a presence. And there is always the appealing side of Jake, the openness of the young man, the sense of wonder as he thinks of what California might really be like, his lovely awkwardness when he reunites with his sister and her family – all facets of character that Kasdan realized from the beginning Kevin could bring off.

'He has energy, lightness, speed,' said Kasdan, 'and at the same time intensity. I wanted the Jake character to have that kind of untamed energy, the reckless, forward movement that has always attracted me to Westerns.'

Neither is there anything wrong with any of the other performances in the movie, all of which are excellent except for John Cleese's Home Counties sheriff who seems always to be on the point of breaking out into a silly walk. Though inhabitants of Torquay may well have become sheriffs of Western towns, Cleese is never going to convince us he was one of them. Otherwise, Linda Hunt's typically splendid playing is the highlight of the supporting acts, making one wish that her role had been more developed. Rosanna Arquette's love interest doesn't give us anything like enough screen time to justify her prominent billing in the movie, being little more than a walk-on role, but she looks as if she means what she is saying about the glories of the unadulterated landscape.

And this is where *Silverado* rates most highly, for it is in its understanding of the old West's physical country that it can fire the senses, much helped by John Bailey's magnificent photography and the clever score from Bruce Broughton. Everything about this film looks right and (musically, at least) sounds right; it is a movie filled with a love and sympathy for its surroundings, but, sadly, it isn't quite enough to make *Silverado* work as a whole, and it is clearly the screenplay that presents the problems. The comings and goings of the four adventurers grow increasingly convoluted, dressed up with dialogue that doesn't always hit the mark. Ultimately, *Silverado* simply outstays its welcome.

But all art feeds on other art, takes from what has gone before, and it is tempting in *Silverado* to identify several strands that seemed to lodge not only in Costner's mind but in the consciousness of his film-makers. Some of them are obvious enough, and not as unimportant as they might at first seem.

In Danny Glover's role as the token black cowboy of the old West we may look ahead to Morgan Freeman's Moor of *Robin Hood: Prince of Thieves*. In effect, these are one and the same role, standing out as they do in all-white landscapes of characters and culture as different, misunderstood, thoroughly good individuals holding on, with difficulty, to a belief in their own moralities and culture. In simplistic terms, we are as unused to seeing a black cowhand in a Western as we are to seeing a black figure in a traditional English story, and one is left with the feeling that both roles may have been introduced more as a response to our current sensibilities than as an effort to mirror the past.

Something of *Silverado* also, naturally enough, would find its way into *Dances with Wolves*. Both films being Westerns, how could it be otherwise? Both movies make much of a stampede, for example – much more, in the case of *Dances with Wolves*, which is also the stampede that stays in the audience's mind. The stampede in *Silverado* also stayed in the mind of the film-makers, for it took over a week to get the sequence in the can. Curiously, there is also the little matter of the hero's lost hat, a feature of both movies, that at least says something about how important fashion accessories were to macho cowboys.

Following Costner's performances in *Fandango* and *Silverado*, Eric Pleskow, chief executive of Orion Pictures, offered the actor his choice of any of the company's scheduled films. Like others, Pleskow had recognized Costner's unusual qualities and the potential for star status. For Pleskow, Costner in *Silverado* had absolutely 'jumped off the screen'.

What both *Fandango* and *Silverado* had done was to provide Costner with an ideal way of working through his actor's adolescence, allowing him to re-emerge as a more sophisticated, adult performer. All that potential of adulthood was about to be realized. Through Gardner's transition from loud college boy to a grown man facing the ghastly dilemma of Vietnam, through Jake's gung-ho wildness into the beginnings of a spark of manhood, Costner had worked his own passage to maturity, and it was time to celebrate his graduation as a screen actor. Now Costner could look back to acknowledge the influence of his own heroes, not the least of whom was the man he would often be compared with – James Stewart.

'*How the West Was Won* is responsible for a lot of what I am,' said Costner in later years. 'The image of the James Stewart character appearing on the river in his canoe has never left me my whole life. I always felt like the solitary guy.'

This, in some ways, was just as well, for his career was radically changing. It is glib to say that, as the chrysalis becomes the butterfly, so the actor becomes the star – glib, but often, in the world of the movies, true. It is a very solitary, and usually unstoppable, process. It was happening to Kevin Costner.

6   Doing Good

In a career that had often been unlucky in the way its lucky breaks turned out, *The Untouchables* was the movie that, more than any other, launched Costner on his truly winning streak. His name was at the top of the film, he had a brilliant supporting cast, superb writer and a director (Brian De Palma) working at the top of his form. For Costner to fall in with this particular movie at this stage of his life was a tremendous boost, and, happily, the attributes that made up the role he was playing were attributes that brought out the fine qualities Costner could bring to it, confirming his rating as a leading actor. Here, Costner was standing up for decency as Eliot Ness, leader of the so-called 'Untouchables' who, in 1930s Prohibition-haunted Chicago, dared stand up against the ganglords ruling the town under the kingship of Al Capone.

Before Costner was signed for the movie, Mel Gibson had been a favourite possible lead (but was held up with the shoot of *Lethal Weapon*), with other sizeable names Harrison Ford and William Hurt in the running. When Costner came up for consideration, he had the personal recommendation of Lawrence Kasdan and Steven Spielberg, but Paramount was uneasy about having so expensive a project resting more or less on an actor who was promising rather than proved; bigger names would have to be brought in for some of the supporting roles.

Sean Connery was an inspired choice for the life-battered cop Malone, but Robert De Niro – the first choice for Capone – thought he would be unable to fit it in to his schedule, and the role went instead to Bob Hoskins. De Niro then found he would be available and offered his services, upon which De Palma graciously insisted that Hoskins should be handsomely paid off, never having shot a second of film, with $200,000.

The industry knew it could rely on De Niro and Connery to bring in dependable performances, and Brian De Palma knew his confidence in Costner would be repaid as the actor played out writer David Mamet's account of Eliot Ness's transformation from a clean-living Clark Kent to a bloody-handed Superman.

'He can take those old Western lawmen lines and make them real,' said De Palma, pointing out that Ness 'goes from this simple Candide character to one as close to Dirty Harry as you can get.'

For *The Untouchables'* producer Art Linson, 'There was no doubt in my mind that Kevin was the best for it. I wanted him as soon as I saw *Silverado*. He looked like a great mid-Western movie star to me.' And, when Linson first met Costner, striding in to the interview sporting a leather jacker, he was immediately reminded of Steve McQueen – a recognition that would have delighted Costner.

In preparation, Costner read extensively about Ness, Capone and Chicago in the twenties and thirties, listened to the reminiscences of an 83-year-old widow of a Capone colleague, and studied photographs supplied by the Chicago Historical Society. There was also invaluable advice from 88-year-old Al Wolff (one of the original members of Ness's posse), and Bob Fuesel of the Federal Criminal Investigators' Association. If Costner wished to refer to other screen portrayals of the man he was about to impersonate, he could look back to the vastly successful TV series of *The Untouchables*, in which the so-obviously serious-minded Robert Stack had played Ness for 117 episodes between 1959 and 1962; there had even been a film (of sorts) made from the series in 1960. Otherwise, it had been left to the little-known actor Phillip R. Allen to play Ness in the 1979 movie *The Lady in Red*.

But however much research Costner had indulged in, when it came to the shoot he often had only his own instincts to fall back on, as this Ness was a Ness that hadn't been shown on screen before – basically, a home-loving, sit-by-the-fire guy, giving his kids Eskimo-kisses as he cuddled them in plump easy-chairs. 'Nobody could tell me how to do that, except myself,' said Costner.

For his version of the Eliot Ness–Al Capone confrontation David Mamet wanted to get away to new territory, pointing out that 'the TV show was more Ness versus Capone and his men; the film is more about the innocent young agent and the old Irish policeman who teaches him how to become a cop'.

Fortunately, Mamet's breakaway from the thrust of the TV *Untouchables* tied in with Linson's ambitions for the project, which sounded pretty worthy – he wanted to create 'a big-scale movie about mythical American heroes'. Linson and De Palma's vision of what the picture should be resulted in them making heavy demands on both Mamet's talent and patience, as they banged the table for rewrite after rewrite. Mamet's ultimate response, as he handed over his final effort, was to happily tell the pair of them to 'Get lost.'

Now, much of the new movie's fate depended on the skill of its writer and director. It was a near-perfect match.

Brian De Palma had debuted as a director-writer with such tasty titles as *Murder a la Mod* (1968) and *Hi, Mom!* (made for a mere $95,000 in 1969), later writing and directing such movies as *Dressed to Kill* (1980), with Angie Dickinson and Michael Caine discovering the problems of transvestism, and the John Travolta vehicle *Blow Out* (1981). As director only, along the way had come the successful *Carrie* (1976), showing his talent for Gothic horror, and the 1983 *Scarface*, an updating of Howard Hawks's 1932 film starring Paul Muni as, to all intents and purposes, Al Capone. Thus, by the time he came to *The Untouchables*, De Palma had some experience of his new movie's theme, if not of the period – his *Scarface* had been moved on to America in 1980. As for his attitude toward *The Untouchables*, De Palma made an unequivocal promise.

'This is a film about good and evil, and my point of view is clear. These criminals are evil, they wreak havoc with other people's lives, and should be put away. In all my films, good triumphs over evil.'

The name of Chicago-born David Mamet also ensured that *The Untouchables* would have a fascinating screenplay – he is a writer who seems incapable of producing poor work, though all his output may not live up to his own high standards. He had already won distinction as a playwright, taking the Pulitzer Prize for his Broadway drama *Glengarry, Glen Ross*. His work for the screen had included his much-praised screenplay for *The Verdict* (1982) which had Paul Newman as a struggling alcoholic lawyer in a brilliantly crafted movie, with Mamet bringing off a fascinating character study as well as an exciting courtroom drama. Later, Mamet emerged as the director-writer of several intriguing works, among them *House of Games* (1987), *Things Change* (1988), and *Homicide* (1991). There is no doubt that *The Untouchables* stands with the best of his writing, even though his retelling of Ness's story parted company with the facts on several points.

The real-life Untouchables (the name given to Ness's staff) numbered twelve, not four, none of them was over thirty years of age or in the employ of the Chicago police-force (strictures waived in the movie), and Ness did not start a family until after he had nailed Capone. Real-life Chicago in the 1930s also contrasted sharply with 1980s Hollywood when it was revealed that Costner was being paid $800,000 for the movie – Eliot Ness's annual salary had been a generous $2,800.

Mamet's concept of Ness marries the man absolutely to his cause and, to an extent because of Ness's low profile in the public imagination, was able to fashion him as if from new. Capone is necessarily much more prescribed as a character, coming to any fiction with all the furniture his notoriety earned him. Though mystery surrounds much of Capone's history (was his real name Capone or Caponi?; was he born in Naples or Chicago?) Mamet had little choice but to retell the story of the gang-leader's brutality. Anyway, by far the more interesting person in the movie is the weather-beaten cop-on-the-beat Malone, who arrived direct from Mamet's imagination.

For both Mamet and De Palma, the casting of Ness was a crucial decision. De Palma argued strongly that they had made the right one.

'He has the straight-arrow idealism of a young Jimmy Stewart,' he said of Costner. 'Very vulnerable. A lot of people who read our script said, "But you haven't made Ness strong enough." ... This is a portrait of a man coming of age. He wants to get Capone. But he wants to get him within the law.'

Art Linson sounded equally sure about his star.

'Kevin had just the combination of innocence, enthusiasm, earnestness and leading-man looks we were looking for. He's one of a small group of actors who fit the bill for middle-American, middle-thirties, leading-man parts. That means Kevin Costner could get very rich.'

There were sure signs during the shoot for *The Untouchables* that this was so. The National Association of Theatre Owners (NATO to the un-politically minded) voted him as its new Star of Tomorrow, a vindication of his achievements that Costner was pleased to accept. The hiccup occurred when Linson wouldn't release Costner from his shooting obligations to go down to collect the trophy. The miffed NATO thought again, and decided to give the prize to an actor who could manage to say thank you in person. If Costner was going to be the Star of Tomorrow, he would have to achieve it without NATO's blessing.

Meanwhile, perhaps what none of those involved in the creation of *The Untouchables* – producers, director, writer – acknowledged, was the way in which Costner's role would consolidate so much of the image that seemed to suit him best. Costner's aura of goodness, allied to Ness's goodness, his willingness to show good and demonstrate goodness, is here almost overpowering. Goodness, contrasted starkly with the grandiose, almost operatic badness of Capone and his cronies, suffuses Mamet's story.

The task facing Special Agent of the Treasury Department Eliot Ness (Costner) is to break the rule of the ganglords running Chicago during Prohibition under the dictatorship of Al Capone (De Niro). Ness's first well-publicized attempt at routing a consignment of whisky ends in embarrassment, after his war-like cry to his men 'Let's do some good', when the consignment proves to be one of parasols. A dispirited Ness is walking home when he meets the gritty Irish cop Malone (Connery), who gives him his first lesson in law enforcement: 'Make sure when your shift is over you go home alive.' We see a troubled Ness comforted by being in the company of his wife and child, listening to Amos 'n' Andy in their cosy, nattily-wallpapered front parlour.

Ness calls on Malone to join him in his fight against Capone, but Malone says he prefers to go on living. Meanwhile, the diminutive accountant Oscar Wallace (Charles Martin Smith) has been sent over to help Ness, and tells him he thinks Capone could be indicted for tax evasion – if only the evidence can be found. Ness doesn't really consider this a viable proposition.

Malone arrives to offer his services to Ness and together, in an amusing scene at the police shooting-gallery, they select the other member of their team, the immigrant Italian George Stone (Andy Garcia). Now, the four men are ready to start breaking into Capone's world. Malone takes them to where a huge cache of contraband liquor is concealed.

'If you walk through this door now,' he explains to Ness, 'you're walking into a world of trouble and there's no turning back.'

Ness's team – soon to be dubbed the Untouchables – begin earning their reputation as crusaders against Chicago's corruption. It is a real threat to Capone. At a lavish dinner-party where he entertains his men, Capone indulges in grisly banter, jokingly lecturing his guests on the importance of teamwork. Using the allegory of baseball to emphasize its importance, he strolls up and down playfully sporting a bat. Suddenly, he brings it down on the head of one of his men. Blood seeps over the perfectly white tablecloth. Capone has brought his point home; his punishment of the weak link in the chain who had allowed Ness his success is complete.

For Ness, his threat to Capone brings real changes. Capone sends his henchman Frank Nitti (Billy Drago) to threaten Ness over the safety of his wife and child, and Ness arranges for them to be moved to a safe house, leaving him free to concentrate on the interception of a delivery of liquor to Capone's men. The Mounties co-operate with the Untouchables in what turns out to be a bloody shoot-out (even eagerly enjoyed by Wallace, who turns out to be a spunky little fighter), and they capture one of Capone's close associates, who knows the name of Capone's bookkeeper but won't tell it.

Malone has his own way of making the guy talk: out of sight, he pushes another member of the gang up against a wall and tells him that unless he delivers the information he wants before he counts to three, the man will die. At the count of three, the man has not responded (for, as Malone knows, he is already dead) and Malone shoots him through the mouth. Inside, the terrified captive squawks that he'll tell them what they want to know. Thinking Malone has indeed assassinated his prisoner, the Mounties' Captain is suitably appalled.

'Mr Ness, I do not approve of your methods.'

'Yeah?' says Ness. 'Well, you're not from Chicago.'

Wallace discovers the name of Capone's bookkeeper, and his accusations result in a subpoena being issued for Capone to appear on charges of tax evasion. Capone wants Ness and his family dead, he wants 'to piss on their ashes'. This scene is smartly followed by a sanctified sequence between Ness and his wife, who has just given birth to his son. But there is much horror to follow. Nitti infiltrates police headquarters, with the help of the corrupt chief, and assassinates Wallace and his prisoner.

An outraged Ness confronts Capone face to face, but Capone tells Ness he has no case against him and, sure enough, the charges are dropped. It seems to Ness that the Untouchables are washed up, but Malone persists in his investigation, trying to pummel information out of his totally corrupt colleague. That night, in his rooms, Malone is viciously shot up by Nitti. He dies in Ness's arms, spitting out his last challenge, 'What are you prepared to do?'

The bookkeeper is captured in the set piece shoot-out at Chicago's Union Station (De Palma and Mamet's sudden excursion into heavily stylized cinematic technique) and the case against Capone is brought to court. Ness has Nitti removed from the courtroom for wearing a gun.

Carelessly picking up Nitti's matches he sees Malone's address scribbled there, and knows Nitti was his killer. Nitti makes his escape but is eventually captured by Ness. Nitti taunts Ness with the knowledge that he will get off the murder rap, and Ness knows he must nevertheless cling to his decency and bring Nitti to the justice laid down by the law. At the last, however, Ness feels that justice to be in his own hands; he throws Nitti from the roof, sending him crashing through the roof of a car below. In Nitti's coat is discovered a list of the jury members who have all been bribed by Capone.

'I have come (sic) what I beheld,' says Ness, but pleads with the judge to swop the jury with that of the court sitting next door. Told that he, too, is in Capone's ledger, the judge complies. Amidst uproar, Capone's lawyer now offers his client's plea of 'Guilty'.

'Here endeth the lesson,' Ness barks at Capone.

Stone takes his farewell of Ness, who looks lovingly at a photograph of the Untouchables, when the four men looked strong, happy, invincible – untouchable. Ness walks out in to the clean light of day, and a reporter asks what he will do when they end Prohibition.

'I think I'll have a drink,' says Ness, and walks off home.

Mamet's screenplay was generously, if blatantly, mapped with emotional signals, not the least obvious of which was the fact that, here, Motherhood is the epitome of everything that is proper and decent, everything that Ness and his crew are fighting for.

There are only three female roles. One is the heartbroken mother of the little girl blown to pieces by one of Capone's bombs, who appeals to Ness as a representative of the forces of good. Biting his lip, Ness's resolve to do his 'good' can only be strengthened by her entreaties. She makes her brief mark as an ordinary, decent, innocent woman, and then resigns from the movie.

Ness's wife is similarly portrayed chiefly as a mother, not as a person in her own right. We never see her doing anything except peering at her Eliot lovingly across a room or snuggling in an armchair with the child he has fathered. In fact, she seems encumbered with children, even going so far as to give birth to a son without having ever troubled to give us any sign she is pregnant. The fact that she is not even distinguished with a name of her own, but is merely known as Ness's wife, points her out as some sort of appendage to Ness, secure in the temple of his home, and a heavily allegorical tribute to Motherhood.

The third female role also goes without a name – the mother of the baby in the pram at the railway station. Not only is she necessary to set up the filmic *pièce de résistance* of the shoot-out, wheeling in the ultimate innocent (a puling, chuckling baby) to become involved in the movie's most explicit conflict between good and evil, but makes the strong, reiterated point that Motherhood is the most easily assimilated, valid and emotive representation of the morals of society. This placing of women is no shallow trick of Mamet's, either, but threads its way through the movie. It is no coincidence that Capone (even when seen with his family) and his cronies are never seen in the company of women. When Mr Capone is around, the nearest we get is a fleeting glimpse, here and there, of blatantly good-time floozies. We may conclude that at least a degree of Capone's sexuality is satisfied by power and violence.

For some, the contrast between good and evil in *The Untouchables* may seem heavy-handed; it is certainly in no degree subtle, but this itself is the cleverest of devices. Most obviously, the cosy scenes of Ness's home-life follow on those depicting Capone and his colleagues. Ness and his family inhabit confined, warm areas, with washes of soft music and misty lighting; Capone is seen in vast open spaces, desolate in himself but surrounded by the opulence of unnecessary luxury. Then there is the contrast of the two men's actual physicality: Capone bloated, smug, and viciously arrogant; Ness lean, loving, uncertain, but increasingly secure in his determination and belief.

This battle between the two forces explodes throughout the movie in moments of violence that carry a real shock, but these are essential milestones that mark an audience's reaction. And the audience involvement could not be doubted. At the death of an evil character, audiences cheered at the triumph of good, no matter how ghastly the end of the villain; at the death of Malone or Wallace, audiences watched in stunned silence. This vindication of De Palma's clear definition of good and evil packed a terrific punch wherever the movie was shown.

The most dangerously contrived and suspenseful sequence of *The Untouchables*, which also serves as Ness's most testing time, in which he steps over from good into something that looks to us very like evil, is the scene at a deserted Union Station. Perhaps the artifice of this scene, the action pulled through in slow motion, is something of an accident. The original intention had been to stage the shoot-out on a period train, an idea discarded because of mounting production costs. De Palma proved himself equal to the challenge.

'Give me a staircase, a clock and a baby carriage,' he called, and proceeded to fashion a piece of film trickery that was a direct tribute to the famous Odessa Steps sequence in Sergei Eisenstein's *Battleship Potemkin* (1925). Mamet regretted its inclusion, but, to a degree, the artifice works.

As the tired mother trundles her baby carriage to the top of the long steps, the main players in the shoot-out take their places, and mother and child become unwilling pawns in the game. It is, of course, Ness who has tried to get the pram, mother and child up the steps and out of the way before the shooting begins, and it is Ness who decides that he has to let go of the pram (at the very top of the steps, of course) if he is to achieve his capture of an essential quarry holding the secrets that will facilitate Capone's downfall. Although Ness has allowed this catastrophe to happen, we are aware that he too suffers through his decision, and could not have forgiven himself had any harm come to the baby – its safe landing is further proof that forces for good are working for him.

These are shades of character that Costner suggests perfectly throughout the movie. Here is a man who starts with a kind of dullness, a flat dedication to his task, tempered almost with a sanctimonious pomposity. Experience, and Malone, change all this, and these graduations are clearly, subtly written in Costner's playing. And he looks good in the movie – the dependable straightness of the nose, the engagingly crinkled ears, the easy smirk, all seem happily in period. And Costner himself had the strongest sense of his character's morality.

'My challenge,' he explained revealingly, 'is to make people like a person who takes a moral stance, who for the first twenty minutes may seem to be a dope, a bore. The challenge is to make people like me ... I'm just looking for the ugliness to surface and then for people to look around and say, "Who is gonna deal with this? Who's equipped and who's willing?" '

Such an assured understanding of his own screen persona not only applies to Ness – we can see that it has paid dividends in so much of Costner's work. The tendency to play the saviour of all that is good and decent in his culture was strongly emphasized in many later movies – not least *Dances with Wolves* (where he is effectively one right-on white man against all other white men, presumably because they have not had the benefit of his hands-on experience of Indian culture) and *JFK* (where he is the voice in the wilderness trying to tear off America's blindfold of gullibility and indifference to truth). Perhaps Ness, more than any other of the characters Costner had played up to this time, has a deal to answer for, for he sets a quasi-biblical tone that was to carry through so much of the actor's work. This is unmistakable in the misty sentimentality of *Field of Dreams*, and provides the strongest undercurrent in many more of his movies.

But however good Costner's performance in *The Untouchables* (and it is very good), there is no doubt that Connery and De Niro give the piece much of its moving force. They give two quite superb accounts of their roles, even if they are very different in style and approach.

Physically, De Niro has all the presence necessary for the villain. Before filming began, he sat down to a solid diet of pasta and potatoes, put on twenty-five extra pounds (a transformation he had performed to an even greater extent for his role of Jake La Motta in 1980's *Raging Bull*), and took $2 million for two week's shooting. The attention to detail was an essential part of De Niro's involvement – even the silk underwear worn by the actor for the movie was bought from the very New York shop Capone had once patronized. In a sense, however, De Niro brings a star status to the film that leaves him isolated, with a dangerous feeling that at times he seems to be acting in a movie all of his own, aggravated by the fact that there is never any real confrontation between Capone and Ness.

It is left to Connery's Malone to truly dominate the picture in the most interestingly written role, to which Connery brings the easiest and most accomplished playing in the company. To Malone falls the responsibility of steeling Ness's resolve, of switching Ness's sensibilities from the pure ethic of goodness to the grey areas of reality. Connery hands over a performance of such professional ease, naturalness, charm and charisma that we are beguiled even by his readiness for killing. We will end up caring for Malone as much as Ness does; it will be Malone's death that marks the real turning-point of Ness's quest for a decent society.

Seasoned, witty and consistently underrated actor that he is, Connery was keenly aware of the freshness Costner brought to the film.

'He has a quality I think is quite refreshing,' he said, 'in that he has an openness. Quite a few of the younger American actors, I don't know what it is, they're more angry than they need to be. But he has more balance, and he has a certain kind of naïvety that he uses extremely well.'

The Untouchables had its American debut on 5 June 1987, taking $1.8 million on its first day. Costing $30 million, the movie would go on to earn around $36,900,000 and, happily, the critical reaction was just as generous.

For Geoff Brown in *The Times* Costner did 'an excellent job. So, in a way, does Brian De Palma: he eschews many meretricious effects and comes to terms with the characters.' The *New York Times* found it 'big-budget, high concept and mass-market ... vulgar, violent, funny and sometimes breathtakingly beautiful and often bloody and outrageous,' while *Variety* especially praised Connery's contribution, 'filled with nuance, humour and abundant self-confidence. Connery's depth strongly complements the youthful Costner, who does grow appreciably as Ness overcomes early naïvety'.

A dissenting Roger Ebert thought the movie 'depends more on clichés than on artistic invention' and decided that, while Costner was 'fine', his role was 'a thankless one, giving him little to do other than act grim and incorrigible'.

Pauline Kael nodded her approval of star and movie. 'At first,' she wrote, 'we wonder how anyone could think that this stiff is up to the job (or that Costner is up to playing the role) … But it's a great audience movie – a wonderful potboiler, like *Pagliacci*.' David Robinson decided that Costner 'is a likeable, laid-back Ness who genuinely appears to suffer at the setbacks and bloodshed of the job', but went on to point out that 'there is never a real sense of confrontation between Ness and his adversary'.

Ness and Capone could never, one feels, have spent even a few minutes together. It is not surprising that Mamet's screenplay has them, here at least, only physically facing each other for a few seconds. What, after all, would they have had to say to each other? They are poles apart: the black villain and the armour-clad hero. And, on a more personal level, so far as the actors were concerned, *The Untouchables* meant very different things to De Niro and Costner.

For De Niro, Capone was simply another role to be thoroughly researched and played. For Costner, at this point in his career, Ness was definitely something more, for identification with this character absolutely emphasized Costner's heroic pretensions. Where Ness stood up for home-life and decency, Costner stood for it too. The image was so convincing that audiences did not question Costner's integrity.

Now, at the same time as receiving the attention he had been professionally demanding for so many years, Costner was personally getting his first real taste of the challenges such fame could bring. The pressures would be on his life with Cindy as well as on his career. The heat was turning up on Kevin Costner, the young hopeful whom Richard Burton had so cosily reassured could make a life both as a decent person and an actor. Staunchly, Costner meant to cope with it all.

'If the adulation you get from being in successful movies is your reason for living, you won't ever be satisfied,' he confessed. 'Cindy was there in the beginning. If I can hold my marriage together throughout my career, that accomplishment will be worthwhile.'

As Costner's professional life was taking fire, it can be no surprise that the woman in his life sometimes felt threatened, not least with the arrival of a first daughter, Annie, just as her father's career was really taking off. Other children followed at two-yearly intervals – another daughter, Lily, and a third child, Joe. Costner suddenly had Cindy as a wife and mother.

Cindy's husband had said that being around a lot of women was one of the major perks of his business, which might have struck home to a faithful wife, sitting back at the house with the children, while her husband seemed to be the centre of everyone's universe. Being a grass widow is a difficult vocation at the best of times – in Hollywood, it's a role that all too often plays out a final scene in the divorce court. If Costner had anything to do with it, there weren't going to be any major marital problems ahead, for his marriage was obviously precious to him. It was also something he tried to keep pretty much apart from his actor's life. Cindy and he didn't mix with film people. Costner didn't party. Whenever he was working close to home, he made straight for it at the end of a day's shoot.

After the early years, there were never going to be the sort of problems that plague so many young couples in the real world: money troubles, job insecurities, mortgages, overdrafts. Materially, Aladdin's cave had opened before them, but it was typical of Costner's style that he didn't emigrate to Beverly Hills, preferring a definitely comfortable but less ostentatious pink hacienda, designed and furnished by Cindy, situated in Pasadena, with the added luxury of a four-bedroom condominium in the California Sierras, to which he could escape when the going got tough. Escaping, over the years, was to grow more important to him.

'If I get a million, $900,000 of that's for my lack of

privacy,' he said. 'I can't be a normal father to my children. We go to a baseball game and have to sit in a booth. Otherwise I'm swamped by autograph hunters.'

The cry of 'too much' may sound a little hollow coming from someone who set out to be a name in films, as if such unwelcome attentions were surprising. What penalties did Costner think fame would bring? Tellingly, so far as Cindy is concerned, he has intimated that 'my wife doesn't always like my success and all the hard work'. At least she had no ambitions to be an actor, which Costner understandably thought might really put the skids under their relationship. He later suggested that his screen liaisons with the likes of Susan Sarandon and Sean Young could be difficult for Cindy – putting the children to bed and knowing her husband was involved, even if only professionally, with another woman – to come to terms with. As for anything happening in such situations, it appeared obvious to Costner that if any of his leading ladies came on to him they were really after one thing – more work. He wasn't the man to take the bait.

The couple also had to cope with the gossipy kindness of articles written about their apparently made-in-heaven marriage, the sort even so ideal a pair as Lucille Ball and Desi Arnaz couldn't extend into a Darby and Joan TV sitcom. Couples told that their marriages are perfect have their own hurdles to jump. Despite the immense value that Costner invests in his family (his parents as well as his wife and children) he's perfectly able to compartmentalize his life, his need, as he puts it, to 'separate things in order to keep exploring who I am'. In this sense, his personal responsibility to Cindy can't be expected to get in the way of his career. Even this blow is softened by having her and the children on location with him as often as possible – a stipulation that quickly found its way into Costner's every contract. But, however hard they work to keep their love together, Mr and Mrs Costner still have all the root problems of the most ordinary people.

'Our lives are certainly full of stuff we never ever bargained for,' says Costner. 'It's not perfect. We're just like anybody. We have those long drives home, like everybody does, where there are silences that are uncomfortable ... life is trying to eat all of us, and you either eat life or you're eaten.'

The necessities of stardom certainly meant there were a few attempts, lurking in the years ahead, to chew up Costner's reputation and spit it out. Cindy was going to have to hold on, and tight, but perhaps Costner's firm delineation of his priorities and values reassured her. After all, it's not every father who confesses that his main ambition in life is to live until his first son has reached the age of eighteen.

7 Houses of Cards

Before *The Untouchables* indisputably established Kevin Costner as a leading figure in Hollywood, there were two more movies, held back for cinema release until his profile had been heightened by the Brian De Palma picture. The first was another curiosity in a career that, aside from the mainstream films, has been full of them – the leading role in one-third of a movie called *Amazing Stories*, which had only made the TV screens in the US, but was given a European release in October 1987.

This time round, Costner's talent was picked up by Steven Spielberg, whose company, Amblin Entertainment, was producing *Amazing Stories*, a portmanteau picture, recalling the glut of such movies that at one time seemed to flood the British market, usually bringing together a group of short stories that always seemed to be by Somerset Maugham. The particular screenplay Costner was signed for was *The Mission*, the only one of the three sequences in which Spielberg was personally involved as director (and it showed) and contributor of the original story, worked into a script by Menno Meyjes.

In common with so many other films Costner has made, *Amazing Stories* quickly vanished in the flood of a market where portmanteau films seemed strangely outmoded. A pity, for *The Mission* is a fascinating piece of work, whatever critics at the time of its original release may have made of it. Certainly, they couldn't agree on its worth. Dominic Wells in *Time Out* found Spielberg's contribution 'is the worst by far: it begins as pulp and sinks into pure slush ... the whole [of the film] is never more than the sum of its parts'. Markus Natten for the *Virgin Film Yearbook* announced that 'the cumulative suspense orchestrated is nullified by an incredible dénouement'. Kim Newman in the *Monthly Film Bulletin* took the moderate view that *The Mission* 'contains the best and worst things in the film'.

But much seems to have been overlooked as this collection of oddball playlets disappeared into the mist of forgotten little movies. Two of the sequences were out-and-out comedies – *Mummy Daddy*, a pretty funny script about a horror movie actor encased in a mummy's costume who suddenly hears his wife is having a baby and makes off for the hospital wearing his ghoulish apparel, and the blacker *Go to the Head of the Class*, a playfully horrific spoof on sour relationships between teeny-bopper pupils and their fearsome teachers leading to black magic, decapitations, and worse – but *The Mission* is in every way the most serious portion of *Amazing Stories*.

An American bomber-crew is preparing for take-off at an English air-base. Respected Captain Spark (Costner) at first refuses to take gunner and amateur cartoonist Jonathan (Casey Siemaszko) on this, his twenty-something mission.

'Are you going flying without insurance?' asks Jonathan, and the rest of the crew are aghast at not taking Jonathan with them. Captain Spark relents, and the crew relax with Jonathan on board, for Jonathan, with his gift for sketching quick caricatures, has what they recognize as 'the old imagination'. Jonathan is happy to draw and dream of his young, pregnant wife.

When Spark's men engage with a Nazi plane, Jonathan is trapped in the gun-turret beneath the belly of the bomber. During the battle the wheels have been blasted away. Unless Jonathan can be freed he will surely be killed during the forced landing. Spark and his men make frantic efforts to wrench Jonathan from the turret, but to no avail. Jonathan realizes what fate awaits him, and bids farewell to the crew.

Now, as the plane breaks up and they have no choice but to bring it down, Static (Kiefer Sutherland) tries to shoot Jonathan, to save him the agony of what is in store, but can't bring himself to do it. Back at base, Jonathan's pretty wife runs on to a grassy knoll and looks anxiously upward, while a conveniently available parson offers what biblical comfort he can over the base's tannoy.

'He shall wash every tear from their eyes,' he promises, ' ... for the former world has passed away.' And the gloriously British line-up of air force personnel scour the skies for news of the crippled bomber.

In horror, the crew wait for the terrible tragedy about to happen, but Jonathan, in a manic bid to marshal 'the old imagination', grabs his drawing-pad and pencils and begins work. Soon, he has sketched the plane that is taking him to certain death, and then – at the very last moment – draws in two plump, patched, orange wheels. He cries out to the captain to try the landing-gear one more time. Hopelessly, Spark meets Jonathan's last, seemingly futile, request, and two plump, patched, orange wheels pop out from the belly of the plane.

It is, of course, a sort of miracle. The plane can land safely. Jonathan is cut free and laid out on the welcoming grass of England in his wife's, and Captain Spark's, arms. As Spark slaps his face to bring him round, so the plump, patched, orange wheels melt, and the ruptured plane collapses.

The Mission manages to pack more good things into its tiny screen-time than many mega-movies. Of course, it's essentially a very artificial piece, and the tight, studio-stage feel to the movie suits it exactly. The grounded scenes are tremendously stylized, while the scenes in the aircraft – where most of the movie takes place – are totally convincing. Splendid special effects, the generation of skilfully built tension, and the groundswell of a score from John Williams, are equally important components of this unjustly neglected piece.

The Mission's thesis is presumably that a belief in the imagination can bring limitless powers. Here, what might easily have turned out a patchwork of calculated whimsy is made real and touching, for we have been brushed with magic. Even Costner's Captain Spark (affectionately known to his men as Sparky) reminds us of the extraordinary talents of a certain magical piano, and there is no harm in that, for *The Mission* is boys' comic-book stuff come to life.

In its heavy emphasis on male-bonding, *The Mission* also keeps company with many other Costner movies. This world, like the worlds of *Fandango, Silverado, The Untouchables, Dances with Wolves* and *JFK,* is a world dictated by men. The fact that in *The Mission* this is made so appealing is partly due to the superb ensemble playing of the actors, all of them giving performances that connect head and heart. For Costner, there is the opportunity to show a great range of ability in a very small span, and it's an opportunity he does not miss.

A much more considerable opportunity offered itself to Costner when Orion, riding high on their successful foray into major film production, gave Costner the chance to pluck any one of their forthcoming attractions as a vehicle that might suit him. It was an artful move on both Orion's, and Costner's, part. For Orion, there was the chance to harvest and exploit a new star at the very point in his career when a major role would be of central interest to the public. For Costner, the movie would not only solidify his new-found leading-man status (at least when it came to mainstream movies, movies that critics would take notice of and people would come to see in great numbers) but elevate him to something like a real star. *No Way Out* was a movie carrying a lot of responsibility. As it happened, the property hadn't been one that Orion had slated for production (Costner did not like any of their choices) but one Costner had discovered and persuaded Orion to take on board.

Robert Garland co-produced and wrote the screenplay, based on Kenneth Fearing's novel *The Big Clock* and the 1948 film of the same name. There, Ray Milland had played the unfortunate hero caught up in a web of intrigue – now to be played by Costner, with the 1948 murderer Charles Laughton now portrayed by Gene Hackman. The 1948 heroine had been the director's wife, Maureen O'Sullivan, replaced for the remake by Sean Young.

There were distinct changes in the updated version that were not always improvements. What had been a neat, skilfully produced thriller, with its suspense played out against the omnipresence of the 'big clock', now became a tale of sub-Watergate chicanery, peppered with a fashionable car-chase, a set-piece adventure sequence at sea (abandoned through lack of money as filming ended, this was substituted only after Costner had made a direct entreaty to Orion's bosses), and some buoyant sex scenes that the makers of the original picture couldn't have got away with. For Costner, though, there was no doubt that *No Way Out* was a brilliant choice; for the film's co-producer Laura Ziskin, Costner was the only choice. She had cast Costner for the lead even before hiring Roger Donaldson as director.

'There was a time,' she explained, 'when there was Redford, McQueen, and Eastwood, but now there's only Harrison Ford and Kevin Costner.'

Donaldson and Costner got on well together, with Costner feeling he was having some real input into the creativity of the movie. When he suggested three players whom Donaldson could use, his ideas were taken up wholesale – a pleasure for Costner on both a personal and professional level. He was not only able to take joy from knowing he was working alongside people he had a fondness and admiration for – there was also the new knowledge that Costner would be listened to, that he could influence what was happening around him. For the moment, this only seemed to have happy and positive results.

Luckily, Donaldson also seemed like the right director at the right moment. His career had taken off with a couple of New Zealand-made features at the end of the seventies, from where he had gone on to direct Mel Gibson and Anthony Hopkins in a remake of a tireless confrontation, the British-made *The Bounty* (1984). What he skilfully achieves in *No Way Out* is the presentation of a more mature, sexual actor than Costner's audiences were used to.

It wasn't only the fact that *No Way Out* would mean another big-budget, high-profile movie in Costner's burgeoning career – this film was also the first that would really put him up front as a sex symbol. Only a few minutes into the picture, the love-making scene between Young and Costner in the back of a taxi presented a Costner audiences had not seen before (except for the few who remembered catching him in *Sizzle Beach*). This was a different move for Costner, who was, naturally enough, nervous when the moment arrived to do the scene.

'What made it work,' he said, 'was that we shot it in real time, without the usual heightening with quick edits ... It was a very difficult scene for me, because it felt very sexy, but it also felt a little bit clumsy, a little uncomfortable.'

According to Costner, Young was sympathetic and helpful. There were those who suggested she was more than professionally interested in her leading man, but he strenuously denied any whisper of an infatuation. An odd by-product of such rumours was that he and Young were invited, as a couple, to present an Oscar at the 1988 ceremony. A speech was pushed over to him which, according to Costner, 'Patrick Swayze and Jennifer Grey ultimately made – about almost fucking on the podium ... ' Costner declined to appear as one half of this 'couple', and thought he'd had his last invitation to the Oscars.

During the cab love-making scene for *No Way Out*, Young told Costner to shut his eyes, kiss her and keep breathing, but he was concerned that now audiences would have some idea of how he made love. Whatever ideas audiences went away with, they were certainly seeing a new, sexier, Costner. For those who wanted him merely to be a sex symbol, *No Way Out* was a good vehicle; for those who wanted him as an actor, it was excellent.

He played Commander Tom Farrell of the US Navy, who begins a steamy affair with a pretty girl, Susan Atwell (Young), whom he meets at an official function. They take off together and make wild love in a cruising taxi. While at sea, Tom distinguishes himself during an excitingly-directed rescue and, on his return, is introduced by his long-standing friend Scott Pritchard (Will Patton) to Defence Secretary David Brice (Hackman). Pritchard is Brice's right-hand man and has persuaded Brice to appoint Tom to oversee liaison at the Pentagon between the CIA and other agencies. Working alongside Tom will be another old friend, Sam Hesselman (George Dzundza) who is now systems analyst for the intelligence unit.

Tom's affair with Susan gathers momentum, and they go away for a weekend out of town together. She tells Tom she is Brice's mistress. Brice calls at her house when Tom is with her. Unhappily, Tom leaves, seen, but not identified, by Brice, who slaps Susan round during a violent quarrel and accidentally pushes her to her death over the banisters.

Brice runs to confide in Scott, who takes charge of the situation, tells Brice they must cover the story up, goes to wipe Susan's place clean, and picks up the negative of a polaroid snapshot of Tom – the image, however, cannot be clearly seen. Scott outlines his master plan to Brice. The quest for Susan's killer will turn into a quest for a yet-to-be-discovered Russian agent whose presence in America has long been suspected by Intelligence. It is this agent who has spent a weekend with the girl and subsequently killed her. When Scott's assassins find the man he will be killed without trial or question. It only remains for this spy – obviously the man in the photograph – to be identified, and the negative is given over to Hesselman, who says his computers will reveal the face of the man within a matter of hours.

Scott and Brice appoint Tom to lead the search for the spy-cum-murderer. Tom, to his horror, realizes the dead girl is Susan, and the depth of the trouble he is in. Scott arranges for Susan's girl friend to be eliminated, as she knew of Susan's relationship with the defence secretary, but Tom, after a thrilling chase, is able to get her away to safety.

Back at the Pentagon, Tom tells Scott he doesn't believe for a moment in the existence of the supposed Russian agent. Knowing time is running out on him, Tom asks Hesselman, for the sake of their old friendship, to slow down the resolution of the face in the photograph. It's his own face, he tells Hesselman. Tom goes on to explain that Brice was responsible for Susan's death, and Hesselman agrees to hamper the computer's progress.

Now, a witness who saw Tom and Susan together during their last weekend arrives at the Pentagon, catches a glimpse of Tom (who manages to slip into a room without being seen by anyone else) and recognizes him. It is now clear that the spy is in the building, which is sealed off. There is no way out, for when the traitor is discovered, Scott will by some means stage his execution.

The troubled Hesselman decides to confide in Scott all that Tom has told him. Scott thanks Hesselman for letting him know, and kills him. But Tom has traced the origins of a jewellery-box belonging to Susan which inexorably links her with Brice. Brice crumbles, admits his role in the affair, and immediately switches the blame for the cover-up on to Scott. In desperation, Scott kills himself by blowing his brains out. As the film ends, we learn that Tom is indeed the Russian agent, and has sought the love-affair with Susan as a means of eliciting top-secret information from Brice. A broken man, Tom walks away from his Russian masters, but they know he will come back to them some time in the future.

Whatever critics thought of *No Way Out*, and it won many good notices, their views of Costner were never far away when the movie had its premiere in the US on 14 August 1987, some two months after *The Untouchables* was released. For Pauline Kael 'Costner has a pleasant air of not thinking too much of himself, and he gives you the impression that he's doing what's wanted of him. Still, this agile fellow who spends the whole movie in movement is the essence of laid-back; he has no inner energy, no kinetic charge.' Less flatteringly, John Simon for the *National Review* decided that 'Costner manages to be both loutish and drab – but that may well be what this age craves in its heroes.'

Whatever sort of hero Tom Farrell is, Costner was fascinated by him.

'It's been quite a challenge playing this character in and around the Pentagon with all these real-life officials in the next room making decisions that affect the country,' he said. 'It was important to me not to cheapen the character. I wanted to maintain a sense of dignity.'

But the perception of Costner's character is made more difficult by the tricks the script plays on him. It is one thing to have Tom behaving as if his sweet world of love had collapsed around him and eliciting our sympathy as he desperately tries to extricate himself from the net closing around him, but it seems a little unfair to expect audiences to hold on to that sympathy when Tom is eventually revealed as the spy. In this case, apparently, he has fallen in love with Susan in cold blood, merely to get his hands on the information she can unlock for him. In its woolly way, *No Way Out* was taking advantage of all the fashionable interest in political chicanery, duplicity and treachery that Americans could stand. Costner realized the film's theme might be linked to the Oliver North controversy raging through America at the time.

'I didn't find Oliver North attractive,' he explained. 'When I watched North's testimony I wasn't looking for a winner and I didn't see one.'

If the links with the Oliver North scandal didn't get home to British audiences, they could look to the John Profumo scandal that had rocked its government, for a similar real-life situation.

No Way Out doesn't exactly advance Costner's ethic of portraying characters that tell us something meaningful and good about the American life – being a Soviet spy isn't the most American hobby. What it offers is the sight of an actor showing he can stand on his own, for this movie is a long way from the strong ensemble work Costner excels at in so many earlier movies – and some subsequent movies, not least *JFK*. However important *No Way Out* may be to an understanding of Costner, he was clearly attracted to the role because he saw facets in the character he could identify with.

'I'm more like Farrell than you'd think,' he admitted. 'Likeable, but full of secrets ... Like Farrell, there's a certain part of me that's very cynical, a part that doesn't like authority. I can work within the framework of authority, but don't push me too far.'

This is not to say that Costner brings the film off all by himself, or that all his work in the movie is equally successful. When he is Tom Farrell the lover, he splendidly conveys the open, ordinarily-randy appetites of a sailor, but he has the advantage of Sean Young's friendly, sexy performance to work with. It is our loss, and his, that she vanishes one-third of the way through the movie. Naturally, after her disappearance the whole axis of the movie shifts from a steaming story about a love-affair to a straight-down-the-line political thriller. The transition, with Tom realizing the horrific changes happening around him, is tremendous – in retrospect, however, is his agony at learning of Susan's death real or false?

Staying with Costner through to the end of the movie are the always excellent Gene Hackman, making Defence Secretary Brice a convincingly nasty piece of work, and Will Patton as the scrubbed, dapper, gay personal secretary Pritchard. Through Donaldson's subtle direction, and Patton's intelligent performance, we get the suggestion that Pritchard's admiration and loyalty to his worthless boss would not, if he got the chance, stop at the bedroom door. But this is a nuance in a movie that is generally free of them; its intelligence lies in its speed and ability to hold our attention by suspending belief in plot devices that don't bear close inspection.

In its hip, easy style, *No Way Out* is marvellously entertaining, cleverly hitching itself to the little army of sub-Watergate thrillers that were proving fashionable. Its set-pieces – the sea rescue and the car chase – seem pretty meaningless in the context of the whole movie, but brought pace and colour, and some exotic locations, to a screenplay that might have been marooned completely at the scene of most of the film – the Pentagon (in reality, Stage 27 at the MGM Studios in Culver City).

There were some losses as well as gains in Garland's updated screenplay. The identification of the murderer, in Jonathan Latimer's screenplay for *The Big Clock*, rested with a character played by delightful Elsa Lanchester (supporting her husband Charles Laughton, as she had through many pictures). Such eccentricity was a little unlikely for a pulsing political thriller of the late eighties, and in Garland's version Tom's fate depends on how quickly a computer can come up with his face.

Ultimately, however, such niceties were incidental. What was at stake here was Costner's central performance. In *The Untouchables*, the movie Costner moved on to after *No Way Out*, he was to play a very different game. The central performance here is buttressed by superb work from two greatly-respected giants of film-acting, Robert De Niro and Sean Connery. In *No Way Out*, where Hackman (another, perhaps less lauded, giant), delivers so laid back a performance that it might pass the unwary by, Costner was, indubitably, starring.

It was an achievement he didn't mean to go back on.

8   The Church of Baseball

So far, so good.

No actor could have complained at the chance of having his name above either *No Way Out* or *The Untouchables*. Orion, relaxing in the knowledge that putting its faith in Costner as a star attraction had paid off, with critics and public, wanted to keep him in its stable. And where most actors, at this crucial time in their careers when a reputation might be made or unmade in the twinkling of a couple of dud movies, might have played utterly safe by going for pictures consumer-designed for mass approval, Costner did the opposite. His attitude, to the unsympathetic, might have seemed self-willed. He chose two movies that nobody in Hollywood was interested in making, about a subject that, according to an innate understanding in the film world, had audiences walking past cinemas in their thousands – baseball.

Hollywood's experience with the game, over the years, had been variable but not without fascinating highlights. No less than Gary Cooper (with whom Costner was constantly being compared) had fronted the 1942 *The Pride of the Yankees*, a biopic of Lou Gehring, the ultimately ordinary American guy who took baseball seriously and made it work for him. Herman Mankiewicz and Jo Swerling's screenplay for producer Sam Goldwyn had won the movie, directed by Sam Wood, an Academy nomination for Best Picture. Two musicals had used the game as their starting-points: *Take Me Out to the Ball Game* (1949), where Frank Sinatra, Gene Kelly and Esther

Williams had danced through some colourful nonsense, and *Damn Yankees* (1958), after the successful Broadway musical, making use of the Faust legend to link up with a modern baseball theme.

In the eighties, Hollywood had stepped up its interest in the game. *The Natural* (1984) based itself on Bernard Malamud's novel and had Robert Redford leading a remarkable cast through a strongly allegorical journey. *Brewster's Millions* (1985) was yet another remake of a very old cinematic chestnut with the dubious advantage of Richard Pryor as a pitcher for the Hackensack Bulls suddenly landed with a vast fortune. *Amazing Chuck and Grace* (1987) relied heavily on winsomeness to make its schmaltzy account of a precocious 12-year-old baseball player's effect on world politics digestible.

Looking at cinema's track record, it had messed with baseball many times, but with no guarantee of integrity, intelligence or success. That Costner was going to take on two new movies based on the game gave Hollywood pause. Before taking these movies on, Costner turned others down, including two 1988 movies with sporting themes – and, from their respective receptions, he seems to have made the right decision. Laura Ziskin had offered him *Everybody's All-American*'s leading role of a hugely success-ful athlete slipping into middle-age and failure: Costner had given way to Dennis Quaid for this one. John Sayles, writer and director of *Eight Men Out*, had tried for Costner to star in his story of the 1919 Chicago White Sox baseball scandal – the downfall of no less a legend than Shoeless Joe Jackson, whom Costner would pay a special tribute to with his second baseball movie.

In some ways, he must have been heading for the two Cinderella projects he finally agreed to from adolescence. In the school yard, and later at college, Costner had been at his happiest playing as short-stop or pitcher. Baseball was something he could do well, that came naturally to him, the inherited American instinctiveness of it taking him over. In his late teens, his body less well-formed than many of his friends, he might not have shown much interest in girls, or they in him, but baseball gave him the opportunity to lose himself in something aesthetically and spiritually fulfilling.

Now, the two movies that used the sport as their foundations, would grow to satisfy him in the same ways. They represent probably the very finest work Costner has done on screen. They provide two utterly fascinating, but very different, aspects of the American myth, and Costner's ability to act as that myth's front man. They are *Bull Durham* and *Field of Dreams*.

It would be accurate to remember that there had, in fact, been another, earlier Costner movie, *Chasing Dreams*, that had him wound up with the sport, but there was never any danger of this being in the same class as the work Costner was now involved in – *Bull Durham*. The movie's credits read 'written and directed by Ron Shelton', but Shelton, basing the screenplay on his own 1979 play '*A Player to be Named Later*', had lived this movie as much as written and directed it. Previously, Shelton's cinematic experience had been as writer and second-unit director for Roger Spottiswoode's *Under Fire* (1983) and *The Best of Times* (1986). Before this, he had spent five years working as a second baseman in the Baltimore Orioles farm system. Through it all, Shelton had loved baseball. With *Bull Durham* he conveyed that love with coruscating success.

In the light of Hollywood's lack of belief in baseball-orientated movies, it isn't difficult to see why Shelton's screenplay was generally cold-shouldered. Costner was about to change his industry's perception, but not until he and Shelton had shown the script all round 'like a couple of Santa Monica hookers'. Finally, Costner held a pistol to Orion's head, giving them a deadline of a few hours to either finally accept or decline the movie. Orion gave in, took on *Bull Durham*, and looked ahead to the $50 million the picture would gross.

For the project to succeed, it was obvious that from the start Shelton, with his tremendous personal commitment to the movie, and Costner, bringing with him the furniture of his growing status, would have to get along – and of that there was never any doubt. Each saw his commitment to the picture reflected in the other, and derived strength from a good personal as well as professional association (a situation that has always brought out the best in Costner).

Shelton's immediate understanding of Costner was that

here was a shy person. They went out for some drinks together, and decided to try out their baseball tactics by spending some time in a batting-cage. It made them feel so good they had the other actors hired for the movie go through the same routine. Once rehearsals began, Costner's shyness didn't prevent him from coming up against Shelton, and the pair had their argumentative discussions about the way the film was going, but their friendship was never in doubt. And this is what Costner insists on always – subjugation of everything else to the matter in hand, the making of a good movie.

On the very first day of rehearsals, Shelton was impressed that Costner seemed to know not only his own lines, but everybody else's, and had his own positive thoughts on the other characters' motivations and statements. Costner also hit a home run before the gathered company and crew – a good omen that wasn't to be disappointed. It helped establish the confidence that he could at least to some degree take pride in his own, no matter how limited, ability to play the sport he was pretending to be a master of. For Costner, it was important to feel he was not merely an actor, a charlatan prepared to take on anything that came his way. It also helped him cope with the responsibilities that accrued from being the film's leading man, hired for a fee of $1.5 million.

'I'm being treated like a veteran actor,' he said, 'and I realized when I get with other actors on the set that they're looking to me, and I can hardly believe that ... Being the lead actor to me is being a supporting actor, because you're the only one who can save a bit player.'

Fortunately, so far as *Bull Durham* went, there were no bit players in need of saving – only a fabulous cast with no weaknesses. Above all, there was glorious Susan Sarandon – the best leading lady Costner has ever had or is likely to play opposite in the future – coming to the movie after wonderful work in such disparate movies as *The Rocky Horror Show* and *Atlantic City*. She recognized the qualities that Costner brought to the piece. For her, *Bull Durham* was 'the best working experience I ever had. Kevin worries about all the right things. That's why he'll be a very good director ... Audiences respond to his value system because they sense that he's an honourable man, a family man, and he is all those things'.

Around the honourable, recognizably decent man, there was also the clutch of great performances from the supporting actors, led by Tim Robbins as the cheerfully randy Ebby Calvin LaLoosh, the ace baseball player with the peanut brain, always looking for a nickname ('Pokey?' suggests his girlfriend). Further down the list there was sterling work from dependable character actors, which even included some wholly charming acting from none other than the real-life 'Clown Prince of Baseball' Max Patkin.

When *Bull Durham* opened to excellent reviews in the US on 24 June 1988, those who should have known what they were talking about inside and outside the film industry were quick to appreciate both the movie and its leading actor.

From the Columbia office Frank Price said that 'After watching Costner in *Bull Durham*, my reaction was "Boy, he's got the kind of strength Gable had." I haven't seen that in years. If you were re-making *Gone with the Wind*, I'd cast Costner. He's the one person who's got the strength to do Gable's role.' For the *Motion Picture Annual*, *Bull Durham* was 'an extremely sexy movie that uses humour and sexual tension, bared souls rather than bared bodies, to turn up heat. Finally given a role that allows him to act rather than behave, Costner delivers the best performance of his career.' Roger Ebert thought *Bull Durham* 'a treasure of a movie because it knows so much about baseball and so little about love. The movie is a completely unrealistic romantic fantasy, and in the real world the delicate little balancing act of these three people would crash into pieces.'

Though enjoying only a limited release outside the US, presumably because the distributors, with some justification, may have considered it offered an overdose of American culture and too much baseball, *Bull Durham* took some $22 million at the box-office – and movie-goers deprived of the chance of seeing it had been done a great disservice. This is not to say the film is not an acquired taste.

Shelton's creation is artificial: his characters do not always speak the way people speak, with their tendency to make speeches, notably Annie's opening comments and Crash's list of beliefs. What we are given here is so stylized as to turn the speakers into their own Greek choruses. But in *Bull Durham* the smile never leaves our faces, and often explodes into laughter – this is the best sort of movie-making, making the world seem a better place than it probably is. It is a movie that is always worth revisiting.

And, though ostensibly about baseball, *Bull Durham* is as much about almost everything else that concerns a human being – growing, maturing, understanding and loving. The scene Shelton sets to enact his thesis is a run-down minor-league baseball team, the Bull Durhams, renowned only for losing games and avoiding crowds and headlines. There is one bright thing on the horizon this season – Ebby Calvin LaLoosh (Robbins) – but if Ebby has been given a thunderbolt for an arm, he has only a ten cent brain. To guide and mature the irresponsible Ebby, the Bulls' managers hire Crash Davis (Costner), 'the player to be named later'. Crash, frustrated by being stuck in the minors for twelve years, is an embittered failure who wants to tell the Bulls what they can do with their job, but he is trapped by his love for the game.

The Bulls' other huge asset is Annie Savoy (Sarandon), a vastly intelligent devotee of the games of sex and baseball, who has made the sport her religion. Annie's understanding of quantum physics, Mayan mysticism, and everything spiritual, embraces the works of William Blake, Emily Dickinson and Fernando Valenzuela. She sees her role as hooking up with one player each season, selecting the guy who will most benefit from her experience and guidance, who will receive what she has to offer in helping him up to the major leagues. This year, she takes an immediate fancy to Ebby, who the managers realize has some 'serious shit' when it comes to throwing the ball – his problem is he can't hit what he's aiming at. Annie's friend Millie (Jenny Robertson) puts her finger on the problem when she explains that 'He fucks like he pitches – all over the place.'

Crash and Ebby's first meeting is a confrontation between them over which one will dance with Annie. Crash doesn't want to put his fists up, but knocks Ebby to .the floor with one blow, introduces himself as Ebby's new catcher, and takes him off for a drink. Annie is glad to see them getting to know each other better ('even if it is only latent homosexuality rechannelling itself'), and invites them both to her home, which includes her private shrine to baseball.

It is time for her to explain her plan to Crash and Ebby. Simply, she can't make up her mind which of them will have her favours and support during that season. This is too much for Crash, who tells her he's not interested in a woman who's interested in 'that boy'. Annie questions his beliefs, and Crash is happy to list them.

'I believe in the soul, the cock, the pussy, the small of a woman's back, the hanging curveball, high fibre, good Scotch, that the novels of Susan Sontag are self-indulgent, overrated crap. I believe Lee Harvey Oswald acted alone. I believe there ought to be a constitutional amendment outlawing astroturf and the designated hitter. I believe in the sweet spot, soft-core pornography, opening your presents Christmas morning rather than Christmas Eve, and I believe in long, slow, deep, soft, wet kisses that last three days. Goodnight.'

Alone with Ebby, Annie begins his education, making him strip off in slow-motion, tying him to the bed and reading Walt Whitman at him all night. ('It's more tiring than fucking,' he complains). Annie gives Ebby the nickname he craves – Nuke.

By the time the Bulls go on a disastrous road tour, Annie and Crash are obviously attracted to each other, but she has completely committed herself to the improvement of Ebby. She gives him a black garter to wear during games, telling him he has been pitching on the wrong side of his brain and that her garter will help restore the balance. Only Crash, who reveals that once, for twenty-one days, he played with the major leagues, stands out on the tour, but at least his relationship with Ebby – who begins to appreciate Crash's advice and maturity – develops.

Ebby takes off on a winning streak, but at a price – by rechannelling his sexual energies and keeping away from the frustrated Annie, who complains she has never had a season like it before ('The Durham Bulls can't lose and I can't get laid').

Ebby is climbing, meticulously obeying Crash's wise advice, but the Bulls have no further use for Crash, and terminate his contract. Annie, too, is in crisis. She storms at Crash that her unhappiness is all his fault, that Ebby is doing what Crash wants him to do. Inevitably, their impassioned argument rises to the pitch of their realizing their feelings for each other, and they lose themselves in each other's love, in long, lingering scenes in beds, bathtubs, and on kitchen tables.

All this seems no answer to Crash, who takes himself off from Annie's bed early one morning, makes her breakfast and leaves a note telling her he's gone to apply for a job as catcher with another team. As time passes, Annie realizes how much she misses Crash. She can't stop thinking of him, can't go to the game with any feeling. It rains. She walks home uphill from the stadium one day when the game has been called off, and Crash is waiting, silently, on her porch. She sits beside him, and we know there is a new beginning. We hear Annie's voice giving us her last thoughts.

'Walt Whitman once said, "I see great things in baseball. It's our game, the American game. It will repair our losses and be a lesson to us." Look it up.'

On the sidelines, *Bull Durham* has many incidental delights – the unlikely but pleasing pairing-off of the much-travelled Millie with bible-toting home-boy Jimmy (William O'Leary); the hilarious antics of the Bulls' managers, putting on a special bad temper in the shower-room to scare the players into action, trotting out on to the field to offer advice about appropriate wedding-presents for Jimmy and Millie; the 'rain-out' that Crash organizes for the pitch they don't want to play – all glorious moments in a movie full of its own strange charm.

Added to these is the sum total of all the actual game scenes in the movie, shot at the El Toro Field, co-owned by the movie's co-producer Thom Mount, and home to the real-life Class A farm team, the Atlanta Braves. They have a real feeling to them that belies the fact we are watching actors playing baseball players playing baseball, and if a movie like *Bull Durham* is to convince on all levels it needs to convince here.

But *Bull Durham*'s particular achievement is not to make a really good movie about baseball. If the heart of this picture is really about the game, much of it must remain impenetrable to the outsider whose knowledge of the sport is severely limited, for whole passages of the film are in a language that seems resolutely personal to baseball itself. What emerges so strongly from Shelton's screenplay is the utter inevitability of baseball to the American ethos, and we see it as a thing of the utmost beauty, symmetry, importance, and relevance.

To the unseeing, it may be that when this movie isn't about baseball, it's about sex, but nothing could be further from the facts. What the film seems to be saying for most of its length is that sex is fun but baseball is crucial. The maturity of Ebby, Crash and Annie, that grows during the movie, proves that this balance can be altered. Shelton and his marvellous players show us that the changes can only come after a deal of pain, transforming what begins as a rorty, smart-edged comedy into a deeply moving experience – the best in movie-making. If Costner was to keep this sort of company in his industry, there was clearly no telling what he might achieve in the future.

'The common thread in each of my films is poignance,' he explained, 'narrative in a movie-world that thinks audiences won't sit still for it. All the camera-work in the world can't disguise that there's no story ... My movies can't be salvaged by a car-chase.'

By sticking to his conviction that good movies begin with good scripts, Costner's reputation was tremendously enhanced by Shelton's talents – enough to make an intelligent observer hope the two will work together again. What Costner and Sarandon did was to take Shelton's finely-honed dialogue (here and there so worked and shaped that he threatens to come on as the Ivy Compton-Burnett of the movie world) and make it spark, even if, as with Crash's firework-display creed, it had all the spontaneity of a well-rehearsed Noël Coward witticism. Interestingly, Costner could not even find fault with the content of Crash's manifesto, including his assertion that 'Lee Harvey Oswald acted alone'.

'He's thought about it,' said Costner of Crash, 'and he's read, and that's what my conclusion is ... Maybe I believe in Lee Harvey Oswald because I can't believe we're so fucking corrupt – maybe I have to believe that.'

In the light of what Costner was asked to espouse a couple of years later in *JFK*, it's a good thing that actors are not always held to their promises. And Costner's absolute involvement with what he had committed himself to in *Bull Durham* could never be in doubt.

'There's a lot of people in the business who don't lose sleep over lines not being right. I lose sleep. I can't even sleep when I get a scene right. It's that passion. They say the industry lacks dialogue. The industry doesn't lack dialogue, it lacks passion ... The guys and women I like working with lose sleep and are scarred for the rest of their lives over certain films.'

Brian De Palma talking to his leading man during a break in
The Untouchables. With his neat haircut, determined nose and
crinkly ears, Costner was every inch the clean-cut hero

The comforts of home, a vital ingredient of so many Costner
movies, typified in *The Untouchables* by a nameless wife,
innocent child, and overbearing wallpaper

Second-billed David Grant seems content to let his sick brother (Costner) take the credit for winning in *American Flyers*, a movie with a beginning, middle and end that didn't quite add up

Sean Young and Costner in their Sunday best at the beginning of *No Way Out*. A few frames later they were stripping off in the back of a taxi

Those who wanted Costner as a sex symbol had to wait for
No Way Out, but Costner was afraid that now his audience
would see how he made love

(*Top*) Much of *Bull Durham* is incomprehensible to anyone not brought up on baseball, but it showed Costner matching his stringy sexuality to good writing

(*Bottom*) As much about a sense of belonging as about baseball, *Bull Durham* featured Costner with a perfect leading lady, Susan Sarandon

9   Home Run

From the start, there was never a doubt as to why Costner gave himself over to the film that followed *Bull Durham* as his second 'baseball' movie in a row, at a time when most other actors would have shied away from becoming too closely associated with a particular brand of sports movie: quite simply, Phil Alden Robinson's script.

Robinson and Costner, coming together for the first time with this project, were kindred souls so far as commitment, talent and intrinsic cinematic intelligence went. Both had also spent a long time on the outside of Hollywood looking in. Before Costner seized on *Field of Dreams* for the perfect gift it was, Robinson had spent seven dispirited years trying to get it off the ground.

'I've been pretty lucky,' said Costner, 'because so many of the movies I wind up doing, like *Field of Dreams*, no-one wants to make. Nobody wanted to make *No Way Out*. Nobody wanted to make *Bull Durham*. And, for the longest time, nobody wanted to make *Field of Dreams*.'

In retrospect, we can only be grateful that the film didn't take off until Costner hitched up with it, for here is a prize example of the right artist meeting the right material at precisely the right moment. But *Field of Dreams* should not have been Costner's next project. For what seems to have been the longest time, Costner had been on the verge of starring in a movie for Columbia. At one point, it had even appeared likely that he would be asked to direct it – a development that would almost certainly have got Kevin Costner, film director, off to a shaky start. *Revenge* was not to be a movie that enhanced anyone's credentials. As plans to put it into production collapsed amidst personal and professional collisions, Costner moved over to Robinson's film.

In a hard-boned industry, getting by with Schwarzenegger blockbusters, superstar quickies and movies with generous lashings of bad language and violence, it probably seemed to some moguls that Robinson, with his penchant for calculated whimsy, had stepped back from a different age. For a writer, he seems to have majored in charm, a difficult commodity to sell in the cut-and-thrust of modern movie-making, where Hollywood's infrequent forced attempts at being charming fall squeakily-clean flat all too often. And, if the leading man of Robinson's seven-year-old screenplay was constantly reminding critics of the old qualities brought to the screen by Gary Cooper and James Stewart (names that would crop up in comparison with even more frequency after *Field of Dreams*), Robinson himself was held responsible for bringing back to films a whole genre of movie-making, most often identified with the work of Frank Capra. Where Robinson was, magic seemed to be in the air.

There had always been a keen sense of wonder and gentle understanding in his work, even in *Rhinestone* (1984), where Robinson had the disadvantage of the movie's star Sylvester Stallone looking over his shoulder at the screenplay and slapping his name on the credits as co-author. Rough and rude *Rhinestone* may have been, with Stallone and Dolly Parton battling it out in a country-and-western treatment of *Pygmalion*, but Robinson's work did have magical leanings, and a strong dose of fairy tale, with its introduction of a Lone Ranger-impersonating-Stallone for the movie's finale.

Robinson's particular style was even more in evidence for *In the Mood* (1987) – also known as *The Woo Woo Kid* – where he recreated, this time as writer and director, the true story of the 1940s 15-year-old Sonny (Woo Woo) Wisecarver, who hit the headlines after running off with a much older woman. Punished by interment in a youth camp, Woo Woo escapes to another older woman and even bigger headlines in better papers. Here, Robinson's especial skill turns what could easily have become a tawdry encounter into something beguiling, in which the protagonists are true innocents at the mercy of a misunderstanding world. Sweetly, at the end of the movie a note flashes on screen from none other than Woo Woo himself, saying he is alive and well and sending everyone his best wishes. Delight was clearly a quality Phil Alden Robinson could trade in. In *Field of Dreams* – his adaptation of W.P. Kinsella's novel *Shoeless Joe* – he traded pure gold. His philosophy, when it came to movie-making, seemed easy enough.

'We live in cynical times. We're all jaded. A lot of our heroes have turned out to have clay feet … I don't believe dreams come true … but it's a primal emotion to want to make the bad good – to hope things will work out in the end.'

For Costner, the enthusiasm generated by reading Robinson's work carried the project through to its acceptance by Universal and producers Lawrence and Charles Gordon. Lawrence Gordon was ecstatic about signing up his star. 'Kevin Costner is one of those people who's so wonderful you hope to God he never changes,' he said, obviously getting into a mood appropriate for the movie in hand.

Pinning his reputation on the quality of the screenplay (never mind its theme of baseball – merely incidental to his decision to accept the movie), Costner's acumen for directing his own career was also proving pretty well faultless. Increasingly, he felt in control of what he was doing, and consciously depended on the support of superb writing to strengthen and extend the persona he had already established as an actor.

'I just believed what Phil wrote from the very first page,' he said. 'The character heard a voice and Phil was able to convince me in the prose of the script that I believed it. It had integrity all over it … It bordered on being schmaltzy, but I think great movies always run that risk of being something else other than being what they wind up being, which is great.'

By the time he signed for *Field of Dreams* – when it had the working title of *Shoeless Joe* – there was no doubt that

Costner's climb was gaining momentum. A sure sign that his name was now filed with the most commercially viable actors in movies was the switch from his trusted friend and agent of many years, J.J. Harris, to the omnipotent Mike Ovitz, the all-powerful head of Creative Artists Agency, Hollywood's most prestigious, zealously guarded, stable of talent.

Beside Ovitz and the gathered forces of CAA, Harris could do nothing but be homespun, but there is no doubt this shift in Costner's status brought with it its own warning signals of being swallowed up by his success, of losing touch with values he had held so strongly. Costner, of course, was determined not to let this happen. The ability to hold on to his growing status was, he felt, in his own gift.

That ability was certainly reflected in the contract he had signed, giving him $2.5 million for his role in the 64-day shoot, mostly on location in Dubuque, Iowa. A condition of that contract – which would reappear with subsequent contracts – was that his family should be with him on location at the studio's expense. He would have their closeness and support during the difficulties of filming, as well as the not inconsiderable support of a magnificent company of actors and technicians.

A hallmark of Costner's success has been always to surround himself with excellent people (in stage terms compare Donald Wolfit, suspected of hiring so-so supporting players in the knowledge that he could easily ride above them, or the host of present-day film stars who make a dubious habit of surrounding themselves with mediocrity), and *Field of Dreams* provided them.

As leading lady, the spiky, gravelly-voiced Amy Madigan was getting her best break in movies to date, assisted by a suitably precocious performance from little Gaby Hoffman, an escapee from the John Hughes kiddie-filled movie-stable, as the couple's sweet daughter. The male support was even more well-seasoned. James Earl Jones, one of the very finest black actors, whose voice had brought Darth Vader to life in *Star Wars* (1977) and *Return of the Jedi* (1983), was on hand to give another totally dependable performance in a role that gave *Field of Dreams* most of its laughs. For his reincarnation, Shoeless Joe Jackson could have wanted no finer actor than the gifted Ray Liotta, whose first appearances in movies, including his murderously attractive husband in Jonathan Demme's *Something Wild* (1986), had shown a sharply defined talent for compulsively attractive acting.

As the icing on the cake, in what must clearly be one of his last major (if supporting) roles, came Burt Lancaster, bringing all the quiet skill accumulated in a long affair with the movies to bear on a gentle portrayal of old age. His casting provided a particular pleasure to Costner, who had long admired the veteran actor's work, and had in so many ways evinced the qualities that Lancaster himself, over the years, fought hard to display on screen. Lancaster's adept turning from the specifically physical roles of his young career to the intelligent reflectiveness of his middle and later years (through *The Rose Tattoo* to the gloriously pathetic *Atlantic City*, with his old, tired man spying on Susan Sarandon rubbing lemons over her breasts – one of modern cinema's most haunting images) was a hint of what Costner's career might hold in the future.

Meanwhile, *Field of Dreams* offered Costner and his players the chance to portray a glimmering vision of how perfect life should be. Like *Bull Durham*, this movie was all about baseball and nothing about baseball. Where *Bull Durham*'s charm lay in its sparky, sexy feel, its carefully prepared speechifying, its knack of wry comedy settling into the hope of a new maturity, *Field of Dreams* had its own message, and delivered it overpoweringly. For some, its appeal was laid on with a trowel and became repugnant, but it took a stern soul not to succumb to the movie's pull and its belief that longings deep in the human heart must be fulfilled. At the core of *Field of Dreams*, certainly for its four leading male characters, is a feeling that too much has been left undone, that a life is incomplete without touching the wildest dreams. Part of the charm of that belief is that the dream can be something as simple as a baseball game.

Perhaps it's no surprise that this movie is underlaid with a strong, possibly unconscious, biblical theme – at least, unconscious in the sense that we don't appreciate this is the feeling while the film is unfolding in front of us. It is a movie moved forward by three stations, three messages carried on the air and heard by our hero. By these words, strongly biblical in their simplicity and authority, Ray Kinsella's progress is motivated. Like some complex riddle, the statements are separate and yet form a whole – and one of the most devastating moments of the film comes in its closing minutes, for only then does Ray realize the real meaning of the very first message he had received. At the end of the movie, he has travelled the way set out, inevitably, by the voices that carry him forward to his ultimate goal. That this level of perfect contentment is reached through the unravelling of so much pain nursed and hidden away through the years only gives the happy ending its heartbreaking quality.

'Emotionally, I believed it,' Costner insisted. 'But it scares people when there's no sex and no violence and no action for an audience as it waits for the ace card to be played. But that ace card can be so magical, it's just like a great love courtship. It can be worth the wait.'

In *Field of Dreams* – moving excitedly forward with its own fluid inevitability – the wait most certainly was worthwhile, if the wait existed, for this is a gentle movie that nevertheless pulses along. From its beginning, we know this is never-never-land, when happy farmer Ray Kinsella (Costner), minding his own business out in his cornfield, hears a voice telling him, 'If You Build It He Will Come.' His wife Annie (Madigan) and young daughter Karin (Hoffman) can hear nothing, but the voice returns.

Ray's thoughts go back to his childhood, his love of baseball, and his fascination with the legendary player Shoeless Joe Jackson; he realizes the voice is telling him to build a baseball stadium on his field, and that 'he' (Joe Jackson) will come. He thinks, too, of his father, trapped in a humdrum job, who had died young, never achieving the dreams he may have had, and Ray doesn't want to go the same way. Annie, not surprisingly, thinks Ray may have gone off his head but tells him if he believes he should do it, he should go ahead. To the consternation of his neighbours and business-like brother-in-law Mark

(Timothy Busfield), Ray ploughs in his crops and builds a perfect baseball diamond, complete with floodlights.

Nothing happens. For a long time, nothing happens, and Annie worries about their finances. Then, one night, Karin tells Daddy there's a man standing in the field. Ray knows at once. He switches the floodlights on to reveal Shoeless Joe (Liotta), ready to play a game with him. Joe has other friends who would like to come play on the field – would Ray mind? For Joe, the field is a miraculous place, where once again he can live for the sport that means everything to him.

'Is this Heaven?' he asks.

'No,' answers Ray. 'This is Iowa.'

The voice has not finished with Ray. A new message is persistently whispered to him: 'Ease His Pain.' After a PTA meeting where Annie confronts the quasi-Nazi elements of a frightful mother (Lee Garlington) in favour of burning the books of the sixties guru Terence Mann, Ray believes he understands his latest message. Terence Mann, spurned by society, had retired from life years before, and Ray is convinced it is his pain he is meant to ease. He puts his argument to Annie, who fully supports Ray's quest. Ray sets off for Boston in search of the lost leader of the sixties.

Mann (Jones) is living in isolation, his real identity unknown, and is not pleased to see Ray, who pleads that they should go to a baseball match together. Mann resists but gives in to his friendly kidnapping, and the two go to the game at Fenway Park. Here, Ray hears the voice telling him to 'Go The Distance' – his third station – and sees the name of a long-forgotten baseball player, who had been privileged to have one inning only in 1922, flashed up on the score screen: Archie 'Moonlight' Graham. It looks as if Mann is leaving him to go on his personal Holy Grail quest alone, until Ray realizes with joy that Mann, too, has heard the voice and seen the message. United in their conviction that something fantastic is happening to them, they make off for the little town in Minnesota where 'Moonlight' Graham settled, only to learn that he died, the community's much-loved and respected doctor, in 1972.

For Ray, it seems like the end of the road, until he looks

around and finds himself back in 1972, and walking down the Minnesota street behind none other than 'Moonlight' Graham (Lancaster) himself. In a poignant exchange, the wistful doctor tells Ray his dream of playing baseball with the greats, with Shoeless Joe Jackson. Mystified as to why he was sent to find 'Moonlight' Graham, and now back in his own time, Ray sets off back home with Mann. En route, they pick up a young boy hitch-hiker who tells them his name is Archie Graham (Frank Whaley). For Ray, another piece of the puzzle has been fixed.

But at home, the farm's finances have resulted in the creditors foreclosing the property. In the field of dreams, Joe brings his dead baseball player buddies to play, and young Archie Graham gets to fulfil his dream. In a heated argument with Ray and Annie over their refusal to face reality, Mark accidentally knocks Karin to the ground. She chokes and is in mortal danger. Annie wants to call for help but Ray looks pleadingly at young Archie, who walks towards them. As he steps over the pitch-line, he becomes Doctor 'Moonlight' Graham, gently bringing Karin back to life. Ray, overcome by what Graham has done for them, realizes the truth – that, now, Graham can't go back into the past again. Happily, Graham accepts the fact, and walks away.

Mark, too, sees the ghosts that were invisible to him before, and is able to share Ray and Annie's dream. Shoeless Joe asks Mann to cross over into the cornfield to join the players. At first, Ray is annoyed that his own efforts have been overlooked – didn't he build the field for them all? Shouldn't he be the one to cross over into the field? But Mann tells Ray his job is to stay home and look after his family, and that everything will turn out well.

'People will come, Ray,' he tells him. 'People will come.'

Mann walks across the baseball diamond into the other world in the corn, laughing and wondering. It is only left for Ray's personal destiny to be fulfilled. He sees his father (Dwyer Brown), dressed for baseball, young, handsome, hopeful, gentle, waiting to play a game with him. The true meaning of the messages is shown at last. 'Build It And He Will Come' had not referred to Shoeless Joe, but to Ray's father. Annie contentedly sees the meeting from the veranda of the house, and moves quietly inside. In the field, Ray and his father take up bat and ball. Beyond, as far as the eye can see, the headlights of thousands of cars come towards them. The people will come.

'I go with good writing,' said Costner, 'and good writing has always served me well ... *Field of Dreams* won't make what a *Back to the Future II* will make. I haven't picked the movies that go over the $100 million mark, but my movies have done okay. I prefer to think of myself as perhaps being not altogether predictable.'

On the set, this was carried through in Costner's fastidious attention to detail, his constant involvement with every aspect of the process of putting the movie together, as James Earl Jones saw from the sidelines.

'Kevin's a unique brand of power,' he explained. 'It's not predictable. He's not after mega-millions or making sure his ego is fulfilled. If you press the wrong button, this man is dangerous ... He's got away with things that a lot of up-and-comers couldn't have.'

Like the man said, his movies were doing okay. Brought in for $16 million, Universal effectively brought the true cost of this particular picture down to a mere $5 million by selling off foreign theatrical rights, and sat back while the film took over $30,000,000 at the US box-office alone. *Field of Dreams* was clearly working its own spell that recalled a time when movies had been slower, less hectic, more homey.

Robinson's screenplay, superbly crafted and with an innate understanding of its boundaries and resources, did indeed recall movies of a day gone by, and not least the name of Frank Capra. There were easy signposts that allowed the happenings in *Field of Dreams* to be compared with those in another great supernatural fantasy, Capra's own *It's a Wonderful Life*. The fact that James Stewart had starred in the one and Kevin Costner in the other seemed another good enough reason to view both actors as, by and large, the same actor. But Robinson's techniques are altogether more complex and searching than those used in the 1946 screenplay by Capra, Frances Goodrich and Albert Hackett.

The Hollywood of the 1940s, despite or perhaps because

of world difficulties, was also rather more geared up for the production of whimsical charm than the hard-boiled Hollywood of the 1980s. For most studios, Robinson's work itself seemed to have been written in a time warp, recalling the world of J.B. Priestley's 'Time' plays and revealing a serious dependence on the sort of beliefs once held by J.M. Barrie. *Mary Rose* is only one of Barrie's works to bear some fascinating similarities to *Field of Dreams* – and then there is *Peter Pan*.

For Peter, as for Shoeless Joe and, ultimately, 'Moonlight' Graham, 'to die will be an awfully big adventure'. In *Field of Dreams*, of course, death is not mentioned as the thing that waits in the cornfield, the place from which Joe emerges into daylight, but this is what *Field of Dreams* is about, insisting on its own belief that understanding can come even after death, that the pains of regret can, even then, be eased.

At best, of course, this is a sophisticated sub-text that may not provide the movie with its most popular selling-point, for, all too often in modern Hollywood, fantasy must equal fun. Robinson does not believe this for one moment. His charm and fantasy would not extend to perpetrating something as unattractive, vulgar or forced as Spielberg's *Hook*, with its overgrown Peter Pan and new belief that 'to live will be an awfully big adventure'. Whereas this sounds like Hollywood fudging difficult issues and substituting its own glib softener, Robinson's movie faces the difficulties without naming them. As pure fantasy, *Field of Dreams* comes over as one of the most honest, deeply moving works about human frailty that have come out of Hollywood for many years.

When the movie premiered during April 1989 the notices for both the film and its star were glowing.

Pauline Kael could not resist inviting her own ghosts to the feast when she told her readers that Costner was 'James Stewart ... and Gary Cooper in their Frank Capra roles; this is the kind of American hero-acting in which only good thoughts enter the hero's mind and moonlight bounces off his teeth.' Phil Hardy became wistful not only about Capra but about *The Wizard of Oz*, linking it up with Robinson's 'sentimental fable – you really can't go back home again – but the dream remains compelling. Like an elliptical Paul Simon song, it conveys both a nostalgia for a time of innocence and a knowing that it cannot be.' Douglas Brode in a review of the films of the eighties saw that, ultimately, 'the movie belonged to Costner, heir apparent to those soft-spoken, but masculine, movie heroes of several generations earlier. Like Costner himself, this film is at once contemporary and classic.'

Not everybody allowed *Field of Dreams* to melt their resistance. Kurt Jacobsen wrote in the *Guardian* that 'the tale is carefully injected with awe, a sense of the miraculous, or such is the intention. I think there's much less here than meets the eye.' Some renamed the film 'Field of Corn', as it manipulated emotions beyond endurance. Certainly it all proved too much for some of the world's most macho males, including Schwarzenegger himself, who rang Lawrence Gordon to say he had not stopped sobbing after sitting through the movie. A prime pitcher for the Mets, Ron Darling, confessed it was the first time he had broken down in tears at the cinema.

Others came away with different feelings. The baseball writer Bill James had some quibbles. Why did Jackson bat right and throw left instead of the other way around? Why didn't Shoeless Joe wear his famous, inseparable black hat? As for the Governor of Iowa, Terry Branstad, he had sat up and taken notice at one of the movie's most telling exchanges. He wanted permission to use Robinson's catchy lines ('Is this Heaven?' 'No, this is Iowa') as the state's tourist-trapping slogan. Robinson didn't go a heap on the idea.

Costner's sometimes forgotten criticism of *Field of Dreams* sounds more interesting since he has himself turned to directing – he wanted it to be a longer film, more measured, to take its own time, rather than that marked out by the studio and the money-men.

'I guess they felt people would get restless and say "Hey, Kev's not throwing a rake at anybody, he's certainly not fucking, so what do we got here, A Care Bear movie?" '

The effectiveness of Costner's performance in *Field of Dreams*, however, was never questioned. Anyone wanting a lesson in seemingly effortless movie-acting need look no further, for the skill is evident. He was a leading actor, but played expertly with his fellow players, a master of ensemble acting. He radiated the decent, ordinary values that people thinking themselves decent and ordinary believe they radiate. Like all the best screen actors, he represented something in us all – in the case of *Field of Dreams*, the numbing sadness that comes through letting those we love go away without having ever really known them.

Field of Dreams may have a hollow centre, but for the time we are with it, belief is suspended. What few seemed to realize was the fact that Robinson's work had effectively canonized Shoeless Joe, awarding him a heavenly, sanctified status he clearly hadn't possessed at the ignoble end of his career. We're not really offered a whiff of scandal in *Field of Dreams*. To make the dream effective, the ghosts must have no dark edges, no murky pasts, no nasty characteristics.

'Is this Heaven?' Joe asks.

Somebody, somewhere, should have told him.

'No, this is Hollywood.'

10 A Monopoly on Passion

One of Costner's most extraordinary failures to get a part he wanted came at the time of David Puttnam's disastrous reign as chief of the Columbia studio. *The Beast of War* was scheduled to be directed by Kevin Reynolds, but it was not only Costner's friendship with the director of *Fandango* that attracted him to the project – he also saw a good role for himself as a Russian soldier fighting in Afghanistan who turns against the Soviet invasion to team up with the Afghans.

Puttnam bluntly informed Costner that he wouldn't consider him for the part, an amazing decision when Puttnam had no star of anywhere near Costner's bankability in mind. For the British boss of Columbia it was Costner's very quality of sympathy that ruled him out.

'You don't have a monopoly on passion,' Costner told him, and left.

In July 1988 *The Beast of War* hit the screens as *The Beast* with a cast of unknowns. It had cost Columbia $10 million, took a measly $96,000 at the box-office, and ended up with a deficit of $9,178,000. The *Los Angeles Herald-Examiner*'s David Ehrenstein hoped that 'When the full story of David Puttnam's period at Columbia Pictures is finally written … a special chapter should be set aside just to discuss *The Beast* … this attempt at mixing melodrama and humanistic "think" piece is most characteristic of the rank incompetence he successfully sold to an ever-gullible Eastern press as artistic integrity.' Perhaps, after all, Costner could breathe a sigh of relief that he had been turned down for this particular movie.

The years would be strewn with films Costner tried for but didn't get, or (increasingly, as his career took off) was offered and didn't want. The outcome of this bargaining weighs pretty well in his favour, for with only one or two exceptions it's difficult to identify a movie he missed out on as being grist to the Costner mill.

The disappointments were many, but they often led on to jobs in other movies when casting directors sensed the actor had something about him and referred him on – this had of course happened early in his career when he tried for *Mike's Murder*. Many other 'might-have-beens' followed. He turned down the chance offered by director John Badham's *WarGames* to take up *The Big Chill*. His efforts to be in Roland Joffe's *The Killing Fields* (1984) came to nothing. There was talk of his being considered for *Mrs. Soffel*, but the leading role went to Mel Gibson in director Gillian Armstrong's 1984 movie about a murderer running off with his prison warder's wife. He passed up the opportunity to star in 1985's *Jagged Edge*, Joe Eszterhas' effective thriller, that instead gave Jeff Bridges' career a leg-up. Sam Elliot beat him to the lead opposite Cher in Peter Bogdanovitch's 1985 *Mask*. Costner was also offered $1 million to play opposite Madonna in the dire *Shanghai Surprise* (1986) – it said something for his subsequently much-vaunted integrity that he didn't sign for it.

More of a disappointment was being turned down, in late 1986, for Joel Coen's 1987 *Raising Arizona*, which instead gave Nicholas Cage's career a terrific boost. On the evidence of Costner's work in *Fandango*, *Raising Arizona* would certainly have made him a star earlier. When the chance came to do Oliver Stone's *Platoon*, Costner didn't hesitate to say no (clearing the way for Tom Berenger to say yes) on the grounds that it might upset his Vietnam soldier brother. Oddly enough, he then tried for *The Beast of War*. He turned down the lead in Alan Parker's 1988 *Mississippi Burning* (William Dafoe accepted); in the 1988 *Betrayed* (making way, again, for Tom Berenger); in the 1988 sports movie *Everybody's All American* (by this time, he had a few ideas about some sports movies of his own);

and in the 1990 *The Hunt for Red October* (leaving Alec Baldwin to play opposite his old partner Sean Connery).

Now, the influence of Puttnam clouded Costner's next project, but at least (if to some regretfully) on this occasion he got to make the film. Whatever other moods this movie would light up, a warm sense of whimsy was not high on the list, for *Revenge*, which had started life as a novella by Jim Harrison published in *Esquire* magazine, took place far beyond the gates of Oz.

From the beginning, however, the star of the picture was in no doubt about the strengths of the story, though he sounded a warning note.

'*Revenge* is a good story, but it's a very tough story to pull off. It doesn't have a conventional ending. It's violent and it's vulgar. It has to be steeped in character. If the people who put it together don't understand that, they're going to make a mistake with that movie.'

A screenplay had originally been prepared by John Huston and his son Tony for producer Ray Stark, who assured the Hustons that Columbia was ready to fall at their feet if Costner was signed for the leading role. There were a few problems along the way. Puttnam wasn't keen to have Stark produce the film, and was unhappy with the proposed budget of $16,000,000. There seemed at times to be no way of clearing the obstacles Puttnam put in the path of getting the movie under way, but Stark's keen interest persisted in a project that 'will be a first for me in its emphasis on sex and violence'. And it was Stark's main hope that John Huston would be sitting in the director's chair.

Huston Sen. had seen one of Costner's films (it's not recorded which) and didn't seem enthused by what he had to offer, instead preferring Anthony Quinn. The Hustons and Costner eventually came face to face at Stark's house to see if an agreement could be thrashed out, but a probably nervous Costner explained to John Huston that, in *Revenge*, he detected comparisons with the stories of King Arthur. This was evidently too much for Huston, who started taking long looks out of the window. Conversation dwindled, Costner left, and John Huston turned on Stark.

'I'm an ill man,' he complained, 'and I don't know how you could do this to me. I've been in this business fifty-odd years and you are telling me that I've got to work with this little guy?'

A helpful Huston went on to suggest that this 'little guy' might be suitable for the part of an AIDS sufferer, and put Costner's name forward for the lead in his son Danny's movie *Mr North* which surfaced in 1988 with Anthony Edwards in the title role. As for the Hustons' involvement with *Revenge*, by the time the movie came to the screen their names were nowhere to be found, while Costner's burgeoning reputation was the film's flagship. Stark was as philosophical about it as possible.

'John and I loved the story,' he said, 'and he wrote a screenplay for me. I really wanted to work with John again, but that was not to be. Sadly, he was too ill. However, I still felt it could be made tastefully.'

Eventually, the project found a new director in Tony Scott, whose name lacked the resonance of Huston, but brought with it much of the promise of his earlier efforts, where Scott had at least shown he could showcase a substantial Hollywood property – David Bowie in *The Hunger* (1983), Tom Cruise in *Top Gun* (1986) and Eddie Murphy in *Beverly Hills Cop II* (1987). What was woefully lacking as the movie began coming to life was the conviction that Costner was happy about being there. The tortuous gestation period of the film's screenplay had been a horror story that seemed to have no ending, coming to a head during the making of Robinson's movie.

'Finally,' said Costner, 'while I was shooting *Field of Dreams* I called up and said, "This is the most awful script I've ever been connected to. It's equally as good a story as I've ever been part of."'

In a last attempt at getting *Revenge* into production Costner brought in Michael Blake and together, over three weeks, they thrashed out a screenplay that Costner pushed over to the studio. They wouldn't have any of it, but at least their star's forcefulness seemed to galvanize them into action. Very soon the picture, rather grandly nominated by Costner as 'one of the first movies about violence', was under way.

Fulfilling at least one of the hopes of John Huston, Anthony Quinn was signed to play opposite Costner, bringing with him over fifty years of film-acting experience. Quinn looked like an obvious choice for the heavy villain of this defiantly Mexican piece – born in Mexico in 1915, he had gone on to a thoroughly distinguished career spanning six decades. Along the way, there had been Academy Awards for his performances in *Viva Zapata* (1952) and *Lust for Life* (1956), and scorching contributions to *La Strada* (1954), *The Shoes of the Fisherman* (1968) and, perhaps most memorably, *Zorba the Greek* (1964), which he had gone on to take into a stage musical version that didn't leave Broadway cheering. Now, he had to cope with *Revenge*, with its unmistakably Grand Guignol storyline.

The film gets off to a shaky start with ex-Vietnam veteran flyer Cochran (Costner) taking his leave of his fellow pilots as he quits the US airforce to find out what real life is like. First off, he plans to take a long vacation with his faithful dog Rocky. We know Cochran is a regular guy when he seems overcome as he bids farewell to his old mates, gives a heart-wrenching salute, and breaks through the mawkish moment by telling his assembled cronies that they are 'pricks, one and all'.

Cochran makes for Puerto Vallarta to rekindle an old friendship with the spectacularly wealthy Tiburon Mendez (Quinn), whose life Cochran had once saved on a hunting trip. Mendez introduces Cochran to his lovely young wife Miryea (Madeleine Stowe), who was gifted to Mendez as a reward for saving her father from bankruptcy. Miryea wants a family, but Mendez, worryingly suggesting that Mexico offers asylum to the most unrepentant male chauvinists, comforts her with his opinion that 'you have a beautiful body, too beautiful for bearing children'. The attraction between Cochran and Miryea is immediate. Cochran makes a present of a jacket to Mendez, and when one of Mendez' dogs playfully attacks it, Mendez picks up the unfortunate beast by its ears and flings it into the swimming-pool. By this early device, we can see that Mendez has a very hot Mexican temper.

Tenuously, Miryea and Cochran try to keep their physical longing for one another under wraps, while Mendez is busily manipulating politicians and taking a dinner guest quietly into another room to have him shot in the head. The sexual tension between the lovers threatens to spill over when they meet on a beach and go back to Cochran's kitchen to make lemonade, but the mood is thankfully cut off by Rocky's insistent barking from the seashore.

At a party celebrating the victory of the politician Mendez has endorsed, the affair begins in earnest. Mendez' henchman, Cesar (Tomas Milian), prowls around the pair suspiciously, but they break away from the throng and make hectic love as Mendez bares his chest and dances the night away. After their first love-making Cochran is thoughtful and worried – as well he might be – while Mendez is soon putting loaded questions to him.

'Do you think my wife is beautiful? Because, a woman like that – I'd do almost anything to keep her.'

This positive statement of philosophy hardly ties up with subsequent events, however, and is only one sign of the seriously unintegrated screenplay.

Cochran telephones his old pilot pal Madero (Jesse Corti) and tells him, 'I think I'm fucked. I think I found love.' Madero is unimpressed enough to advise Cochran to make for the border, but the besotted Romeo is indecisive and soon once again makes love to Miryea. She begs Cochran not to leave her, and they plan to escape for a weekend together, all of which is known to Mendez who has had his wife's telephone tapped. Mendez seems to give Cochran a last chance of escape when he asks him to fly with him that weekend, but Cochran refuses, saying he is going to spend some time alone in his cabin. At the airport, Mendez gives Miryea a last valedictory kiss on the forehead.

Together at last, the lovers ride off, making love in the jeep, making love in the river, making love in the warm, cuddled comfort of Cochran's cabin, while Cochran grows closer to Miryea by explaining what being in Vietnam meant to him; 'Just killing things you didn't mean to, when you hadn't thought it out.' Inevitably, Mendez and his gang of thugs break down the doors. Rocky is despatched by a gun, Cochran is savagely beaten, and Mendez confronts the terrified Miryea.

'You want to fuck?' he snarls. 'You'll be fucked fifty times a day before you die.'

He slashes a knife across her face, and has her taken to a whorehouse, where the madam is told to give her two grams of heroin each day, and to 'give her to the world'. Meanwhile, Cochran, thrown from a car and presumably left for dead, is found by the passing peasant Mauro (Joaquin Martinez), who takes him home, where he is restored, partly by means of Mexican witchcraft, to health. Now, his one quest is to discover Miryea's whereabouts. He meets the terminally-ill horse-trader Texan (James Gammon), with whom he develops a close relationship, but Texan dies. Cochran buries him, inherits his money and his gun and puts up in a hotel where a third-rate rock star (Sally Kirkland) is also passing through.

Amador (Miguel Ferrer), a friend of Mauro's, visits Cochran and tells him Miryea is still alive. Back in his room, Cochran tells his story to the blowzy singer ('Phew,' she replies, 'for a second I thought you were gonna say you were gay'). Amador returns with the news that Miryea is in the whorehouse. We see her stabbing the loathsome Ramon (Luis De Icaza) who is about to rape her. Cochran and Amador break into the brothel where Cochran punches the madam in the face when she refuses to tell him exactly where Miryea is being kept.

Cochran knows the time has come for him to face Mendez. He ambushes his enemy, who suggests that 'perhaps we both deserve to die'. Mendez needs Cochran to ask his forgiveness for taking his wife from him, and Cochran, after some inward struggle, does so. Mendez tells Cochran that Miryea is now in the convent. Overcome by emotion, Mendez is obviously unable to ask forgiveness of his young friend, and rides off alone.

Cochran bursts into the convent where Miryea lies dying. She rallies, recognizes him, and they kiss.

'I love you,' he tells her. He folds her in his arms and carries her from the convent. She whispers 'I love you' and dies. The image we are left with is that of the convent silhouetted against the reddening Mexican sky.

'*Revenge* is shocking, vulgar, a bit of a fall from grace,' said Costner. 'But I have no problem in playing a man who isn't likeable, as long as I understand him. You don't have to have a snow cone at the end of every movie.'

In fact, there is never a real problem with Cochran being likeable, merely with the utter stupidity of what he does in allowing himself a love-affair with the wife of so venomous a creature as Mendez. Lumbered with his apparent lack of basic survival intelligence, Cochran provides little that an actor can build on, though Costner is quite effective in the scenes of anxiety before embarking on the lustful game that will set the tragedy rolling. Madeleine Stowe only begins to spark in these shared moments opposite her leading man; otherwise, she is of negligible interest, and all but vanishes from the story after the fateful night in the cabin.

Quinn's remarkably threatening masculinity, a virulent example of an attractive septuagenarian, dominates the screen effortlessly where he can – hardly difficult for an actor with a renowned and insatiable sexual appetite – but, like Costner, he is laid low by the lurid screenplay, devoid of believable situations, flavoursome leading characters and passable dialogue. When all else fails, it might be agreeable to look beyond the actors to the glorious Mexican landscape, but even as a travelogue *Revenge* is a failure. So many scenes are washed out with a rosy glow that this Mexico becomes, like the film it finds itself in, characterless.

The main pleasures of *Revenge* come from Sally Kirkland as the singer holed up in a low-dive hotel, and James Gammon in the marvellously touching guise of the clapped-out horse-trader, spitting up blood but determinedly carrying on. When these two are in the frame it looks as if they may have wandered into the movie from another sound-stage.

There is an overall sense of opportunism about this film that may even be apparent in its title: what, after all, is this revenge? At the end of the story it is clear that Cochran has been unable to take his particular revenge on Mendez. Mendez' treatment of Cochran and Miryea may well be the only true revenge we are offered, a revenge against illicit love. Of course, there may be layers of meaning at work here that director Scott understands better than his audience, or that he himself does not begin to recognize. In this way, we may begin to see why Mendez merely has Cochran beaten up rather than killed – presumably, this is a revenge tempered by the niceties of deeply-bonded male friendship. But here, too, there are difficulties all along the line. We never understand why the relationship between Cochran and Mendez is so close, and feel saddened that Cochran's life should be so empty that the first thing he wants to do in the world outside is visit so ghastly a person.

If there is an act of vengeance here, it is surely the moment when Mendez crashes in on the love-making of Miryea and Cochran. In this centre-piece we are merely given a scene of sickeningly grotesque violence, made none the less disagreeable because we are probably expecting it. It is here that *Revenge* reveals itself as nothing more than a penny dreadful wrapped in a highly expensive Hollywood bow. Nobody on the creative side of the movie seemed to realize that such extremes of violence must, to work, have a relationship to character and meaning. Another (and this time British) film from this period, Peter Medak's *The Krays* (1990), contains several equally stomach-turning examples of man's inhumanity to man, but there the acts are rooted in an intelligent screenplay that, for some tastes, may even go too far in explaining the gross actions.

No such attention to detail mars the progress of *Revenge*, over which Tony Scott presides with a sophistication that seems to have been borrowed from one of the violent exploitation movies of Peter Collinson. With *Revenge*, what you see is what you get – there is nothing more there. If Costner was into making good movies that contributed something worthwhile to cinema-goers, or enriched their perception of the world, this was a crass mistake.

Unsurprisingly, *Revenge* opened to no chorus of praise. In *Village Voice* Gary Giddins thought it 'idiotic' and told his readers that, by the end of the showing he attended, 'those … who hadn't run for the exits were giggling uncontrollably'. Mat Snow for *Empire* considered the film 'nasty, brutish and, at two hours, far from short ... Certainly, the ideas, such as they are, should never have left the page.' At least Costner's part in the affair was given a welcome of sorts by Nigel Floyd in the *Monthly Film Bulletin*, who found the actor 'revealing a darker, more dangerous side to his increasingly complex screen persona ... [his] performance provides a solid dramatic core for a narrative that otherwise lacks both momentum and force'.

Perhaps it was John Harkness in *The Film Yearbook* who delivered the most deadly review of *Revenge*, citing director Tony Scott as 'the whoring technician par excellence', making films which 'create an image of a man who has no ideas and no soul'. Here, Harkness discovered 'a film destroyed by ambition. It wants to be an existential story about the price to be paid for love in a corrupt world. It wants to be a John Huston movie'. (And can leave audiences wondering how it might have turned out in these circumstances.)

When the mostly disparaging reviews had been read and forgotten, enough people flocked to bring in well over $15 million at the box-office. Nevertheless, *Revenge* may have been most notable for a financial deal agreed in a little hotel in Cuernavaca, Mexico, during the shoot, over a meal of guacamole and taco chips. The discussions concerned a film Costner wanted to make called *Dances with Wolves*.

For the moment, however, Costner was fronting a picture that had done little to advance his career or reputation.

'Movies are like a trial,' he said. 'You assemble all of the information that you can and try to make a judgement. If, when I do a movie, I understand all the information, and I think the movie represents something, I'll do it.'

11 Orson Welles with No Belly

Michael Blake's friendship with Costner had not ended with *Stacy's Knights*, even though their careers had gone off in completely separate directions – to huge success (in Costner's case) and a notable lack of it (in Blake's case). Try as he might, Blake had not been able to break through into the big time as a screenplay writer, and was wondering if he would ever get a bite of the Hollywood cherry. He poured his frustration out at Costner, berating the industry that had forbidden him his big chance. He may have expected Costner's sympathy, but didn't get much. Slapping him up against a wall, Costner told Blake that maybe his lack of success was his own fault; if he came up with the goods, his luck would change.

It says much for Costner's feelings for his friend that it was then Costner himself who immediately took steps that would transform Blake's fortunes, while not exactly diminishing his own. He seized on an idea Blake had nurtured for a long time – the story of a lone US army officer who becomes enmeshed in Indian culture at that crucial time in American history when the acquisitive white man was about to plough the Indian back into the ground that had once been his own. When Blake described the scenario to his friend, Costner disappointed him by saying it sounded less like a movie than a novel, and that Blake should go away and write it.

'I had to choose between getting a job and writing a novel,' explained Blake, 'and I chose the latter. When I was writing I was broke and I couldn't pay the rent, so I got in my car and drove around to different homes – and I wrote the first three or four chapters in Kevin's.'

Blake began work on the book. Having reshaped his ideas into a prose narrative – much of it written when he was lodging with the Costners – Blake took the result back to Costner who looked at it and told him he must go away and rewrite it as a screenplay. In such a way, the seed for *Dances with Wolves* was sown.

Costner's influence on what Blake had written – for both book and film – cannot be overestimated, for Blake has confessed that the story's hero, lonesome Lt John Dunbar, was based on Costner, inheriting the formidable qualities that Costner obviously liked to think he possessed. That such a proud, resilient personality should be fictionalized in a Western film was also no coincidence, for since his childhood exposure to James Stewart, Gary Cooper, John Wayne and all the proud riders of the genre, much of what Costner thought he stood for had come from the Western. After *Silverado*, he had even suggested that he might be the only person in Hollywood who could revive the genre. On Blake's side, there was the feeling that, having come up with the material, Costner was the one person in American film industry to bring the project to life. The fact that Kevin Costner was in fact an actor, not a director, was unimportant. The burgeoning movie was so close to Costner, and seemed so remote to so many established directors, that it looked inevitable: Costner was about to become his own director.

Blake's life-long interest in cowboys and Indians had done a flip when he read *Bury My Heart at Wounded Knee* by Dee Brown, an extraordinarily powerful indictment of America's misunderstanding and consequent mistreatment of the native American. Suddenly, after reading Brown, the excitement and simplicity of cowboys and Indians took on a different meaning, and America's history didn't seem like something to crow about. If Blake could harness his fascination with the savage annihilation of the Indian people to a Kevin Costner movie, he would be a privileged person – for Blake's perception of how America had become America could hardly attract more attention than when wearing the Costner ticket.

For his part, Costner determined that the movie simply

had to be made, but even the strength of his name in the industry didn't have studios begging to be allowed to pick up the bill for it. The financiers' faces fell when the word Western was mentioned, for the imagery and magic of the old West had obviously lost its box-office potency, the costumes and paraphernalia of the Western movie's heyday stacked away in the dusty back-rooms of old sound-stages. Why didn't Costner lift up his head and look around at the debris of movies that had tried, in recent years, to rejuvenate the Western – and failed? Hadn't he even featured in one of the most expensive and ill-advised of recent attempts – *Silverado*? Then, there had been the stinging lesson of Michael Cimino's extravagant stab at breathing life into the Western – *Heaven's Gate* – a production so profligate and critically scorned that it practically wiped out its studio. So, what would *Dances with Wolves* have going for it that these established duds had not?

'Integrity' might have been a reasonable answer, but hardly one to overcome the hard-headed industry accountants. The screenplay Blake and Costner waved at them threatened to last well over three hours, in itself enough to frighten away many a prospective backer. There was also the fact that Costner wanted the Indians' dialogue spoken in their own language, with subtitles for general consumption. Most studios would have fallen over themselves to acquire a Costner movie, but the intrinsic doubts surrounding *Dances with Wolves* blinded them to the opportunities it presented.

Eventually, Orion (for whom Costner had proved a winner in *No Way Out* and *Bull Durham*) came together with the British-based Majestic Films in working out a 50-50 financial support for the new picture, making up the $17 million budget. By the time the buzz had got around that *Dances with Wolves* might actually work and (even more seductively) make a lot of money, Costner was far less keen on the movie becoming just another product of a studio's assembly line. The best thing about having secured Orion and Majestic's help was that the companies now stood back and let Costner get on with making his film, up to a point.

'No one wanted to make this movie at the point that I had it,' protested Costner. 'I think this is everything a movie should be, so I didn't care ... I don't know what kind of director I can be, but I do know my story. What I'll lack in sophistication and camera moves hopefully I'll make up for in story and rawness and honesty.'

Costner's personal involvement with the project was as intense as could be expected of any actor-director leading his own troops into the forefront of cinema. Claiming the movie very much as his own, he set up his own production company, Tig Productions, remembering his grandmother, whose loving nickname had been Tigger. He then reasserted his belief in the film by putting $2 million of his own money into it and, later, when shooting ran behind schedule and the bills started mounting, forfeited his salary until the movie showed a profit. He need not have worried he would not see his money. A year after *Dances with Wolves* was released it was estimated that Costner would make as much as a personal $50 million from it.

At night, he had a recurring dream of playing a part in Custer's Last Stand, which vied with his other recurring dream, where he found himself heroic at the sinking of the Titanic. Had he been making a movie about the fatal ship, there is no doubt he would have been the last to go down, saluting, faithful to the cause to the very end – as his character in *Dances with Wolves* had to prove. For Costner, as so often before in his career, it was a case of going for the right idea at the right time, no matter what advice he might pick up along the way.

'I like to think that I would do the smart thing in my life,' he said, 'and I think that the smartest thing in life is that, when you run across something good, you move towards it.'

As co-producer of *Dances with Wolves*, Jim Wilson – another old friend of Costner's reunited after directing *Stacy's Knights* – was to find the movie a testing experience, but an exercise that would pay splendid artistic and monetary dividends.

'It seemed to be something that we so much wanted to do ourselves,' he explained, 'without any interference whatsoever from the studios. And, basically, Orion and Majestic let us do just that. They're just supportive, and there's no-one here bothering us ... just us two knuckle-heads out here on the prairie making a movie.'

This was one way of looking at it. The fact was that, behind the scenes, Orion and Costner were growing increasingly unhappy with one another. Costner resented the financial pressures Orion were putting on him; the company that had given Costner so many of his chances in cinema was discovering, if it didn't already know, that in the film world there is no such thing as gratitude. By the time *Dances with Wolves* was shooting, it looked as if Costner and Orion would be parting company. They did, Costner switching his allegiance to Warner Bros.

Orion's nervousness was not without cause. The logistics of making *Dances with Wolves* were considerable, the expenses colossal, the risks – even with Costner's name on the marquee – enough to excite the Hollywood grapevine into declaring that *Dances with Wolves* would be Costner's downfall, his 'Kevin's Gate' (an unkind comparison to the disaster of Cimino's *Heaven's Gate*). Costner, went the whispers, was having a bad attack of overreaching himself; he was so caught up by his own roaring success and his sense of clout in the industry that he thought he could direct and star in an epic Western and turn it into a box-office winner. Not a little excited at the prospect of the new boy's fall from grace, the rumours of flop rumbled on.

One of Hollywood's main doubts may have been about the movie's entire ethos, that the white man had despoiled and stolen the Indians' land, and had subjugated, where he could not annihilate, the Indians' culture. To the white man, the Indian was nothing more than a savage, an impediment to progress. America had then gone on to build its own success on this rape – hardly a message that modern-day America could swallow with ease. For a society racked by its involvement with Vietnam, and the subsequent (and, if a later Costner movie was to be believed, linked) downfall of John Kennedy and other leading political icons, the message was bound to be disturbing.

That Blake's screenplay sets Dunbar up as the one white man apparently prepared to approach, assimilate and identify with the Indian way of life, is no coincidence – especially as, here, John Dunbar equals Kevin Costner. Having come to personify so much of home-town, clean-living America, Costner was about to plunge a dagger into the very heart of his own culture, and, being Costner, get away with it. Meanwhile, those around him seemed less concerned with the difficulty of Costner's message than with the mechanics of what he was beginning.

'A lot of people said it's crazy for him to attempt first time out as a director and star, that he should have picked something that's more manageable,' said Wilson. 'But he's always up for a challange. He loves it. If you say, "You can't do it", well, he'll probably try it. No fun if it's easy, I guess.'

This time around, there were no other strong names in the cast to buttress the box-office potential – this was going to be a movie that people came to see because it was, simply, a Kevin Costner movie. As his leading lady he might have had the pick of Hollywood's leading actresses; Mary McDonnell was not a name known to movie-goers. He had been looking for an actress with a lined face, who appeared to have experienced some of the pain of life. It was a promising sign that Costner as director knew what he was doing, as was his decision to cast native American actors in the Indian roles, resisting the temptation to pick actors who looked as if they had been plucked out of some casting directory. Again, Costner's feelings were supported by the casting of such actors as the unlikely-named Graham Greene as Kicking Bird, and Rodney A. Grant as Wind In His Hair, both of whom were striking discoveries for mainstream cinema. As the movie came together, Costner was in no doubt about what he wanted this – his self-confessed 'love-letter to the past' – to be.

'It is a fact that we committed genocide in this country, and we have chosen to ignore that fact. We like to point to South Africa or Hitler. We are aware of what other people have done, but we tend to ignore what we have done to the American Indian. They're gone ... We turn our back on it. But we destroyed a people and a culture to get what we wanted.'

Blake and Costner had, of course, not been the first to paint a sympathetic picture of the Indians. Over the years Hollywood had made several, often quirky, attempts to bring some real understanding and sense of perspective to an industry where all too often cowboys and Indians equated good and evil. In 1950 James Stewart, Costner's ubiquitous precursor, had fronted Delmer Daves' *Broken Arrow*, battling alongside Jeff Chandler to reach an understanding with the Apache. In 1950, however, the movie had lost its edge by having white actors in some leading Indian roles, all talking well-drilled Hollywood English. Other movies offered different views of the Indian, sometimes suggesting that while the Indian was indeed a person there was still some truth in the fables that had made them the enemies in countless Hollywood B-Westerns.

As late as 1970, in *A Man Called Horse*, the Sioux were remembered as the perpetrators of the cruel Sun Vow, under which Richard Harris endures the most horrifying torture, which we nevertheless understand is an integral part of the Sioux mores. In its effort to give a fair and more kindly picture of the Indian, *Dances with Wolves* may itself not be completely blameless in the way it divides them into goodies (the Sioux) and baddies (the Pawnee). Here, the Sioux are almost playing cowboys to the Pawnee's Indians. Some historians have pointed out that, in real life, the Sioux was a notably warrior-like race, systematically reducing the Pawnee, their arch-enemies, from around 12,000 to a mere 2,000 between 1830 and 1875.

Costner's role as director included marshalling the massive forces involved, up to 600 individuals, many of them Indians with absolutely no understanding of English. Blake's dialogue for the Indian characters had been translated into one of the Sioux dialects, Lakota, by Doris Leader Charge, who also played Pretty Shield, and acted as the movie's language coach.

As always with extras and bit-players, Costner was considerate but firm. When they turned up on set not knowing their business he told them they would only be letting down their race if they failed. Costner and Cindy's commitment to the reputation of that race was further proved when they gave $120,000 to set up a permanent Sioux Indian exhibition at the South Dakota Cultural Heritage Centre in Pierre. The thrust of the exhibition, mirroring what *Dances with Wolves* had to tell, traced the rise and fall of the Sioux people, the legend of the Ghost Dance, the white man's conquest and the retreat of the Sioux to life on the reservation.

Besides the difficulties of working with such large numbers of actors, so many of them non-English speaking, Costner was also presented with that perennial danger to any performer – working with animals. One of the main reasons South Dakota was eventually selected as the movie's location (Texas and Oklahoma having been discarded) was that it was home to the biggest privately-owned buffalo herd in the world – 3,500 beasts belonging to Roy Houck – as well as having the bonus of several reservations from which Costner could select his extras. Of the 108-day shoot, the buffalo hunt, the great set piece of the movie, alone took eight, with Kevin Reynolds – Costner's old friend and director of *Fandango* – brought in to oversee its filming.

It was over a hundred years since the white man had ridden wild with the buffalo, a heart-stopping, thoroughly dangerous, pursuit. Refusing to hand these sequences over to his stand-in, Costner again displayed the brilliant horsemanship and courage that he had shown in *Silverado*. Enduring a heavy fall from his horse during the shoot, he got himself straight on to another horse and hurled himself back in to the movie. For Costner, as well as for Dunbar, the spirituality of encountering the buffalo engaged his whole being. In a movie that is especially about man's relationship with animals, this was just as well.

When filming began, it was as much of a family affair as Costner could make it. As was *de rigueur* for a Costner film, he insisted his everyday life should be maintained as much as was feasible during the shoot. Bill and Sharon were brought out to stay at nearby Rapid City, and often turned up to watch their son at work. Those watching them watching their Kevin noted they seemed proud and bemused by turn, and some detected a formidable strength of character in Jim that he seemed to have passed on to his actor son. Meanwhile, Cindy busied herself in wardrobe and was charged with a last-minute effort to round up a number of period wagons, the acquisition of which had been overlooked. The children's presence was commemorated by having them appear as the offspring of the white settler family beset by the Pawnee.

Other events during the filming of *Dances with Wolves* showed that Costner had not lost touch with reality. His · kindness was still evident. When the husband of his hairdresser died, he helped out with funeral arrangements and expenses. His business acumen was also functioning well, with Costner taking advantage of the proved business skills of his brother. Dan and he learned that gambling was to be legalized in Deadwood, South Dakota, and wasted no time in being among the first to offer the new pundits a glittering casino of their own, buying an old property and converting it into the 'Midnight Star' – shades of Linda Hunt's bar in *Silverado*. Michael Blake's screenplay, on the other hand, had none of the complexity and nuances of Lawrence Kasdan's work for Costner's earlier Western, as his utterly simple tale unfolded.

In autumn 1863 Lt John Dunbar (Costner) lies in the Union army field hospital awaiting the amputation of his foot. Determined that he should not lose it, Dunbar struggles back to his men and, figuring he is going to die anyway, takes a buckskin horse across the Confederate lines in a vain, brave attempt at suicide. As a reward for his bravery, his foot is saved, and he asks to be sent to the frontier – 'I want to see it before it's gone.' He takes the buckskin, whom he names Cisco, with him.

Reaching the garrison of Fort Hays, the last major outpost of Dakota, Dunbar receives orders from the broken, diseased Major Fambrough (Maury Chaykin) that he is to travel to the further outpost of the realm, Fort Sedgewick. In the company of the flatulent, filthy peasant Timmons (Robert Pastorelli), Dunbar makes off on the 150-mile trek, only to discover that Fort Sedgewick has been abandoned. Dunbar decides to remain there alone until reinforcements arrive, resolving to restore the garrison to its former glory. Timmons leaves, promising to tell the army of Dunbar's decision, but is shot down with arrows and scalped by marauding Pawnees. The prior occupants of the fort have also died in the Indian country. Now, nobody knows anything of Dunbar's whereabouts.

Alone, Dunbar is entranced by the extraordinary beauty of the country, and starts recording his days, his thoughts, in a little journal. 'The country is everything,' he writes. 'There can be no place like this on earth.' A lone wolf, with milky white socks on his two front feet, begins regularly to visit Dunbar, sitting and staring at him from afar: Dunbar christens him Two Socks. Along with Cisco, Two Socks is Dunbar's only companion.

Weeks go by before Dunbar sees his first Indian – the medicine man of the Ten Bears band, Kicking Bird (Graham Greene), who had wandered away from the Indian settlement and come upon Fort Sedgewick by accident. Startled at the sight of a naked white man, Kicking Bird flies back home, eventually telling Chief Ten Bears (Floyd Red Crow Westerman) of the stranger's presence. The Sioux debate the inevitable arrival of the white men. The young brave Wind In His Hair (Rodney A. Grant) decides to ride out to see this particular stranger for himself. Slowly, a bond develops between Dunbar and the Indians, as Dunbar mimes a buffalo for them, and eventually discovers they have recognized his actions, speaking their own word for buffalo – 'tatonka'. The Sioux are anxious to know how many other white men will be coming.

Just as Dunbar's love of the Sioux way of life grows, so does his love for Stands with a Fist (Mary McDonnell), a white woman brought up by the Indians after her family were slaughtered by the Pawnee. Her remnants of the English language are revived in helping Dunbar and the Sioux communicate. At the time of the coming of the buffalo – essential for the survival of the Sioux – a bridge of understanding is crossed, and Dunbar becomes a whole person for the first time in his life, certain and at peace with himself, as a Sioux. John Dunbar had not been sure of who he was. Dances with Wolves (as his Sioux friends have named him) has no doubts, and leaves the fort to live with the Indians.

But the white man's progress cannot be stopped. Dances with Wolves marries Stands with a Fist, but all know their days of contentment are numbered. Kicking Bird, knowing that an end to their peace is near, asks Dances with Wolves how many white men will be coming.

'There will be a lot, my friend,' he answers, 'more than can be counted ... It makes me afraid for all the Sioux.'

As they prepare to move to their winter camp, Dances with Wolves remembers his journal, left behind at the fort, and knows he cannot leave it there to fall into white hands, for it will lead the army to Dunbar and the Sioux. He rides off to retrieve it, promising to return as soon as he can.

At Sedgewick, the army has already arrived. Thinking Dances with Wolves an Indian, the soldiers lift their rifles and kill Cisco. Dances with Wolves' treatment at the hands of his one-time comrade captors is rough, for he is branded a traitor and told he will be sent back to Fort Hays to await trial. Two Socks appears, looking down at Dances with Wolves as he is taken away by wagon; the soldiers take pot-shots at the wolf, who stands his ground and is killed. Wind In His Hair and a party of six Sioux warriors attack the wagon, killing the soldiers and freeing Dances with Wolves. Back at the camp, Dances with Wolves is filled with a ghastly foreboding that now the army will seek him out relentlessly, and, with him, the Sioux.

Sagely, the aged Ten Bears soothes him. 'The man the soldiers are looking for no longer exists,' he explains. 'Now, there is only a Sioux named Dances with Wolves.'

Columns of soldiers, their progress led by Pawnee scouts, move closer to the Sioux day by day. Kicking Bird and Dances with Wolves part with the exchange of pipes. Dances with Wolves tells his friend he was the first man he ever wanted to be like. The water-stained journal of Lt John Dunbar finds its way back to Dances with Wolves. As he and Stands with a Fist join the exodus from the winter camp, Wind In His Hair triumphantly declares, from his pony on the edge of the canyon overhead, his friendship for Dances with Wolves. A wolf moves across the shape of the moon and howls as the Sioux move away to whatever fate awaits them.

Dances with Wolves is a work on a huge canvas, but to see it as an epic is surely a mistake. The breadth of it all is easily understood through Dean Semler's photography and John Barry's score, for both have the measure of a gargantuan enterprise. As with *Silverado*, *Dances with Wolves* is completely at one with its sense of landscape, but it remains a highly personal film, as much about Dunbar's finding wholeness as an individual as it is about the downfall of an old civilization. Even the flatness of Costner's delivery, often completely expressionless, works in the film's favour, for we know we are listening to very private thoughts, allowed the privilege of hearing what Dunbar confides to his journal. The journal itself assumes a life of its own, to be desecrated when it falls into the hands of the uncouth white men, now Dunbar's enemies as much as the Indians. Restored to him, in its tattered, sodden state, the journal has become Dunbar's bible.

On the level of rolling entertainment this is a movie that works splendidly, if slowly, but it carries its message ostentatiously, with an air of righteousness that is ultimately repugnant. As a study of a small group of characters, most of whom happen to be Sioux, it may seem more pungent than any of its predecessor movies, but even on this level the characterization is facile.

It is also a curiously uninvolving picture. Perhaps it is inevitability that blunts the senses at the deaths of Cisco and Two Socks, but these sequences simply fail to work, possibly because the feeling our emotions are being manipulated prevent them doing so. Mary McDonnell does what she can with the heroine, but this is a stock character who, in good old Hollywood tradition, seems to be there merely to give Costner support and the chance of some wet-eyed acting. And are these Indians so very far removed from their predecessors who rode through hundreds of Tinsel Town movies? Have Blake and Costner really cast such blazing new light on them that our understanding is forever altered? Was Costner naïve enough to believe that, for the first time in its history, America was going to have to face up to the fact that it had built itself on the charnel-house of the Indians? This is either a marvellous naïvety or an embarrassing sense of over-importance.

When *Dances with Wolves* opened to acclaim in the US on 9 November 1990 (a reception repeated on its UK release of 8 February 1991) the box-office takings immediately dispelled any doubts as to the movie's popularity. During its first week's run, US cinemas on average took in some $69,000. In its first ten weeks, the film took over $81 million. Critical huzzahs, and some hefty brickbats, showered the movie, with the more perceptive of critics beginning to question the whole industry of goodness that seemed to have sprung up around Kevin Costner. The thrust of their argument undermined the image so many Costner admirers over the world took home with them. Pauline Kael, for one, did not mince her words, either about Costner or his monster movie.

'A nature-boy movie, a kid's daydream of being an Indian,' was Kael's offering of a put-down. 'The movie ... is childishly naïve ... It isn't really revisionist, it's the old stuff toned down and sensitized ... This epic was made by a bland megalomaniac ... [Costner's] the boyish man of the hour ... the Orson Welles that everybody wants – Orson Welles with no belly.' Costner's response to reading Miss Kael's comments was to say some very ungracious things about her, perhaps overlooking the sensible attitude actors should have to their press notices: ignore them or accept them, whether they be good or bad.

There was more criticism, much more. Barbara Lippet saw in Costner 'a kind of new-age hero – half John Wayne, half Shirley MacLaine ... Perhaps it's also this oddball combination of buffalo-stomping masculinity and soft spirituality that women find so appealing.' Another authoritative American journalist, Richard Schickel, thought that 'Dunbar is an almost too perfect example of the new American male, that improbable beau ideal who has been created out of recent feminist fantasies and the failure of certain old-fashioned masculine dreams.'

Despite the dissenting voices, it seemed that awards were inevitable. Waiting in the wings were the Golden Globe Awards for Best Motion Picture Drama, Best Screenplay and Best Director, though the industry's greatest laurels were of course reserved for the Oscar Awards of 25 March 1991 when *Dances with Wolves* walked away with seven trophies – for Best Adaptation, Best Cinematography, Best Sound, Best Editing, Best Original Score, and – the final accolades for Costner – Best Director and Best Picture, the latter award presented by Barbra Streisand. At the end of the evening, only one coveted award had escaped Costner, for Jeremy Irons had been pronounced Best Actor for his role in *Reversal of Fortune*. Costner wasn't piqued.

'I haven't won much in my life,' he announced, 'so this last month has been very good for me. It's a great night … not the greatest of my life but certainly a great highlight of it, and a great moment that no-one can ever take away from me. My life, though, is bigger than the movies.'

Those who had studied Costner's life and career up to this point did not underestimate what he was telling his industry. The importance of what Kevin Costner had demanded of Richard Burton – could he be a good man and be an actor? – had stuck with him over the years. Now, before his gathered peers, Costner reiterated his values.

'How will I keep my ego in check?' he told them. 'Well, it matters to me what my friends think of me, what my parents think of me, and I think that's a very good way to guide yourself.'

Then, refusing to be drawn as to whether he and Blake would be making a sequel (Blake elsewhere having intimated that he was writing one) Costner, Cindy and their party made off for a celebratory party at the Columbia Grill.

Some other of Costner's pronouncements at this time didn't endear him to his fellow-workers. At a ceremony for the Independent Spirit Awards Costner used the occasion to strut on the platform and criticize the sort of film Hollywood was, in general, turning out, describing it as an 'incomplete, half thought-out piece of shit.' Presumably, he exempted *Dances with Wolves* from this accusation.

That same month, the Native American Producers Consortium reckoned there were around forty films slated for production that highlighted the plight of the Indians in the history of their country, including movies in which Robert De Niro and Robert Redford were to appear. No doubt not all would see the light of day, but it may just be that Costner's movie had done something to open America's eyes to the tragedy of the Indian – or, more prosaically, to its commercial potential in Hollywood. Costner nursed no doubt as to the importance of *Dances with Wolves* on his fellow-man's psyche. 'I think the movie is hitting Americans in the solar plexus, right in the stomach,' he claimed, himself realizing how difficult it had become to walk down an American highway knowing that by rights it should be Indian territory.

At times it seemed unclear whether Costner was making a Western (perhaps a contradiction in terms when the whole thrust of the picture is to show how the very Westerns it seeks to revive were founded on an absolutely false premise) or a soft-focus documentary about the downfall of the American Indian. For some, the contest to discover what the film actually was proved too much: 'ideologically correct and a little self-satisfied' (David Fuller, the *Independent*); 'of sentimentality there is too much, and the final sequence when the white men inevitably rear their heads and raise their rifles so fraught with tears and peril as to be exhaustingly melodramatic' (Angie Errigo, *Empire*); for *Time*, Costner was 'the hard-riding scout bearing Hollywood's message of what America thinks it was and hopes it can be again'.

Convinced that the whole spread of his original film should be released, Costner supervised the cut of the full-length *Dances with Wolves*, which failed to excite movie-goers as the abbreviated version had. If Costner wanted his movie to be compared with the very great, very long films of history (Gance's *Napoleon*, Lean's *Lawrence of Arabia*) his wishes didn't altogether come true, as some critics pointed out they had got the full message the first, shorter, time around. The years will tell how effective the message has been.

12 Two Kevins, Two Robins, and a Race to the Finish

When it came to the movie version of *Robin Hood, everybody* – critics and audiences alike – agreed that it was altogether splendid, and probably the finest work its star had ever achieved. Though there had, early in production, been troubles between the star and his director, and there had been those who lamented the fact that everything seemed under-rehearsed and done on the wing, there was generous praise for the completed picture, its fantastically swashbuckling leading actor, its witty, colourful villains (including a delicious Sheriff of Nottingham), its Academy Award-winning score from one of Hollywood's great *émigré* composers, its Academy Award-winning sets spectacularly recreating medieval England, the whole washed in translucent Technicolour.

From the censors, there had been only one quibble; the love scenes between Maid Marian and Robin (described by the publicity department as 'six foot four of British manhood'), which were so charged with sexual urgency – though nothing actually very physical happened between them – that it looked for a time as if its certification might prevent it from becoming one of the most appreciated and critically lauded 'family entertainment' movies of our time.

Not, alas, comments about Kevin Costner's version of the Robin Hood legend, but Errol Flynn's 1938 edition, mounted by Jack Warner for Warner Bros at a then top price for the studio of $2 million, and a movie that has stood the test of time. The story of Costner's much more mightily expensive and critically mauled account of the tale is less happy, but fascinating in what it tells us about the state of modern film-making in general and Kevin Costner in particular.

Mel Gibson was one of those originally offered the role in the production company Morgan Creek's first major film, but turned it down because he didn't want to work in tights so soon after playing Hamlet. When Costner picked up on the part, there were those who said it was because he wanted the money – a straight $7 million for his name on the credits – or because he thought it would be light relief after the rigours of *Dances with Wolves*, or because he was persuaded into the project through his old friendship with the director.

Probably, a little of all these are true, and Costner considered he could make it into the heart of English myth (hadn't he already licked its American equivalent?) with the help and understanding of an old friend and a reputation that was riding high. Later, Costner claimed he made the film 'for a lark'.

As for hiring Kevin Reynolds, whose friendship went back beyond the making of *Fandango*, as the movie's director, this looks something like Morgan Creek's setting a sprat to catch a mackerel. The company's executive producer James Robinson sank $37 million of his own money into the project, so was not likely to sit back and let the film work itself out. The screenwriters (Pen Densham, who came up with the original storyline, and John Watson) also nailed their colours to the mast as producers. When Costner signed the contract to star in the movie, it seemed the guarantee of a great critical and popular success. In effect, it was the start of a race to the finish of almost nightmarish proportions.

The unexpected problem that threw the movie into immediate panic was the sudden rush all over the film world to take a new look at the Robin Hood saga. Everywhere Morgan Creek turned it learned of other production companies setting out on a retelling of the legend. Inexperienced as Morgan Creek was, it knew one thing for certain – there was only going to be room for one

Robin Hood movie, and it had better be theirs.

At one hilarious stage there seem to have been four or five versions lining up for production. Ultimately, only one other pulled through, to be produced by Twentieth Century Fox. Deprived of the current top shot of the cinema, Fox signed the up-and-coming Irish actor Patrick Bergin, fresh from playing Sir Richard Burton in *Mountains of the Moon* and Julia Roberts' murderous husband in *Sleeping with the Enemy*, as their Robin Hood (or Hode, as they had it). Bergin, a one-time library assistant who had been acting for a mere seven years, had been one of those originally considered for the Morgan Creek production. He had decided to accept Fox's contract after a book about Robin Hood fell on his head in a bookshop. Looking over the wall at the Costner shoot, Bergin crossed his fingers and declared that 'last year was a graveyard for that sort of big-budget film'.

To make the production of the two competing movies into a real race it was essential that they should be shot almost simultaneously, and this was done. To both companies it seemed essential that their baby should be first out of the womb, that the second film would only limp into view at the box-office when the first had had its chance to establish its grip on the public consciousness. Time, ever a precious commodity on the film set, had a heightened importance here. When Morgan Creek's shoot began at Burnham Beeches in Buckinghamshire on 8 October 1990, Kevin Reynolds was left in no doubt by the Morgan Creek money-men that he had to bring the movie in on a 100-day schedule. For the producers, it was imperative that their product should reach the screen on America's Memorial Day weekend at the end of May. It actually opened in the US in mid-June.

From the beginning, Reynolds was put in an almost impossible position. On one hand, here was his first genuine opportunity to establish himself as a front-rank director of a mainline movie, a chance to break away from his reputation as the director of smaller, artier films. Having an almost alarmingly brief shooting schedule imposed on him was disadvantage enough for his first stab at the major league, but he had also been brought in so late in the day – a matter of weeks before shooting began – that there simply was not time for him to live and breathe and investigate the possibilities and question the style of what he had been handed by the writers.

Costner, however, was absolutely sure of him, and made positive noises.

'It's a pretty big statement,' he said, 'but I believe Kevin Reynolds will be one of our greatest American directors in the next ten or fifteen years.'

And this was a director who absolutely believed in going along with himself, at least so far as *Robin Hood: Prince of Thieves* was concerned. He made it clear he hadn't seen the Errol Flynn version that everybody kept telling him about, and wasn't going to make a point of seeing it, or any of the others that had been made about this man who very possibly had never even existed. Watching the movies that had gone before would certainly have kept Reynolds busy for a day or two.

Before Flynn, the most noted Hollywood version was the great (and silent) movie written and produced by, and starring, Douglas Fairbanks, in 1922. Between these and the two 1991 efforts there had been an amazing variety of filmed Robin Hoods, including Warner Baxter's cowboy Robin in the 1936 western *Robin Hood of El Dorado* (there were several Wild West Robins during the 1940s, among them Gene Autry). Frank Sinatra had come up with a tribute of sorts in *Robin and the Seven Hoods* (1964), as had Italian and Russian film-makers.

Britain, naturally enough, had made its own definite contribution, including two excellent television series: 165 half-hour episodes starring Richard Greene and, later, a more modern Robin from Michael Praed, succeeded by Jason Connery, whose father had also played Robin opposite Audrey Hepburn in the 1976 *Robin and Marian*.

This is a movie that those suffering from an excess of the romanticism of the usual Robin Hood offerings can turn to, with a magnificent performance from Sean Connery (far surpassing Costner) in a film that was at the time largely ignored. There is no glamour about this story, and a marvellous matter-of-factness about the enterprise. In a moving final scene, Marian gives poison to herself and

Robin. *Robin and Marian* is not a film that thinks their story is a lark.

Earlier, wonderfully leafy and atmospheric but basically trite, some British versions had Richard Todd blown up to cinema-size for Disney in the 1952 *The Story of Robin Hood and His Merrie Men*, with Don Taylor following two years later in *Men of Sherwood Forest*. Richard Greene made the transition from TV to film with the 1960 *Sword of Sherwood Forest*. Whatever the faults of any of these movies – and many of them had their share – they had at least worked out their own style and flavour.

So far as the new Costner movie was concerned, there wasn't time for Reynolds to thrash out ideas with the screenwriters or producers, who hopefully dubbed themselves the 'three musketeers of the film world'. The fact that two of the producers were responsible for the screenplay made any criticism of their work a little awkward. Worse, there was no adequate time for rehearsals, and this constriction came up against Reynolds' way of working, which was often to shoot and re-shoot scenes using new dialogue and different angles until something ended up in the can that seemed right. Now, those looking on were sometimes puzzled as to exactly what sort of film Reynolds was trying to make.

There was also the problem for Reynolds of working alongside his old friend, now Hollywood's hottest property. Their meeting for *Prince of Thieves* was on a very different level from their collaboration on *Fandango*, when neither had had much of a reputation at stake, or when Reynolds had come up trumps for Costner as the second unit director on *Dances with Wolves* responsible for the fabulous stampede sequence.

This time round, Reynolds was given the job of directing a man who had just emerged as his industry's most sought-after property, with all the strength and determination this gave him. This was a newly-charged, highly confident Costner, a man coming to terms with knowing he was at the centre of other peoples' success, whom Reynolds had to cope with. It was an experience that would destroy the friendship they had enjoyed together, but then, the vicissitudes about to be endured would have tested the most cemented relationship.

By the time shooting began, some of the leading roles were not even cast – and, when they were, were sometimes cast badly. At best, the company looked global. Morgan Freeman, lately from his award-winning role in *Driving Miss Daisy*, was signed to play the Moor who has no part in the original Robin Hood story; Alan Rickman, the highly intelligent and acerbic actor whose credits included praised performances on stage in London and New York and playing the villain of *Die Hard*, was slotted in as the Sheriff of Nottingham; Christian Slater, a Brat Pack survivor, wound up as Will Scarlett. Leading lady Robin Wright was obliged.to pull out of the movie at the last moment, since a pregnant Maid Marian didn't altogether fit in with a story-book romance, and Mary Elizabeth Mastrantonio was hastily pushed into a dress in her place.

When casting was completed, the problems were just beginning. The day before he faced the cameras Costner took a look at his costumes and refused to wear them, leading to the removal of the unfortunate costume designer and his replacement by John Bloomfield, for whom the movie became something of a personal bad dream.

As for Reynolds, he began work by making it clear that so far as he was concerned he was not interested in making a medieval *Raiders of the Lost Ark*, but the writers had served up a hotch-potch of ideas and styles that seemed to be an attempt to do just that. The sheriff, for example, was now heavily into black magic as administered by Geraldine McEwan's fruity witch Mortianna. Costner, however, let it be known that all was going ahead with his knowledge and approval.

'There's scope for horror and there are dark forces to contend with,' he reported. 'I had many discussions with the writers who were receptive to the changes I wanted making. I found the sub-plot between the Sheriff and Mortianna most intriguing, and wanted to develop this dynamic further.'

Reynolds, too, seemed to go with the new roads this story of Robin Hood travelled.

'I'm well aware of the fine line I'm skirting between cartoon romp and gritty drama,' he confessed. 'I'm trying to take the larger than life aspects as far as I can go while staying within the limits of believability. But the contemporary feel makes these well-recorded events less archaic. I instinctively felt this was the right avenue to take as I'm convinced people spoke then very much as we do now rather than in poetic prose.'

There was also the nagging reminder that, after all, Robin Hood was a very English man, and that Costner had a very pronounced Californian drawl. The actor's own intelligence told him as much, and he made noises about wanting to play Robin with a voice that was as English as he could make it. He declared he was willing to fall 'in line with the writing which suggests Robin was the first terrorist. I'm also attempting an English accent because I didn't want this to turn into a United Nations of dialects.'

A vocal coach was drafted in, and set about making Costner's good intentions reality. How successful he would have been may be in doubt (remembering Dick Van Dyke's excruciating squawk in *Mary Poppins* and Cary Grant's embarrassing Londoner in *None But the Lonely Heart*) but time simply ran out on him, and the coach disappeared, while those in charge made comforting but meaningless noises.

From James Robinson came the delightfully quotable commandment: 'Have Kevin Costner play Kevin Costner. We'll fix it at dubbing stage', followed by John Watson's hopeful pronouncement that the movie had 'an interesting blend of voices'.

Then, there was the weather – English weather. When the filming was not halted by heavy rain, it was hampered by suitably eerie mists, and a persistent cold. As the cast and crew limped through the shoot, they grew more dispirited and confused as to exactly what they were supposed to be doing. Sometimes whole days of filming were lost, as when an attempt by Reynolds to film Robin's return to England by boat had to be abandoned – a blow to Reynolds who has a great talent for the spacious understanding of landscape (it is no coincidence that he is a disciple of David Lean). This sequence was eventually directed by Costner himself, returning to the Seven Sisters cliffs near Eastbourne to shoot one of the loveliest moments of the movie, and a sequence in which Costner really does seem to be playing Hamlet. Meanwhile, Reynolds bit his lip and made obliging noises to the press.

'In the course of this production,' he said, 'I would have to say that Kevin has been a real stand-up guy. He's been a trouper.'

From Costner, the doubts as to what he had got himself involved in were soon less well hidden.

'I've had the pulse of every movie I've ever worked in,' he said. 'I've known when they were right, and I've known when they were going south, but I don't know what will happen with *Robin Hood*. If *Robin Hood* is a successful movie, I will be very, very happy. It will never change that it was not a great professional experience.'

One of the brighter moments of the shoot was the day that the film's uncredited surprise actor turned up to deliver his couple of lines for the movie's final scene. Sean Connery had agreed to play Richard the Lionheart (the first time in a long career, he made it known, that he had ever played a gay role) on the strict understanding he would be home in time for tea and that his fee of $400,000 would be given in full to the Scottish Educational Trust.

Meanwhile Patrick Bergin's Twentieth Century Fox *Robin Hood* was drawing to a close on location at Peckforton Castle in Cheshire, its director John Irvin having come in first at the finishing post. Content at least to have finished first, Fox issued the movie with some timidity, which would certainly have been misplaced if it hadn't been for the Costner mega-movie coming up behind it. For Fox's *Robin Hood* was not negligible.

The moist-voiced Bergin took a little getting used to as Sherwood's hero, but managed to look like a particularly alluring insurance salesman. Some blame seemed to attach to him for simply not being Kevin Costner, and the praise the picture got (when it got any) was faint. There is precious little dash about Bergin's Robin, who eschews any attempt at swashbuckling, while the Merrie Men are an eminently forgettable bunch. The sense of camaraderie is therefore fatally diluted in the forest scenes, though there are strong performances from the other leads, including a spirited Marian in Uma Thurman and a guest appearance from Edward Fox doing the equivalent of Sean Connery in the Costner version, making what he can from a few minutes as a patently psychotic King John.

Hybrid, unexciting and sometimes laughable (a careful eye will identify soldiers with arrows implanted in their chests long before they react to them) this *Robin Hood* is nevertheless an enjoyable movie that has suffered badly by becoming 'the other' *Robin Hood* of 1991. Its marvellous sense of place and atmosphere is maintained throughout – this forest actually looks as if it might be Sherwood – and the feeling of medievalism is not confused as it is in the Costner film.

And there is something very appealing about Bergin's Hood that Costner misses. Bergin never gives anything like a starry performance, but he is perfectly in tune with the film, and his gentle charm suffuses Robin's character. This soft quality of Bergin can also bring moments of real enchantment, as in the closing sequence when Robin and Marian marry. Here, everything combines to make the most enchanting finale, with the springing into life of the spring flowers on Marian's head-dress a lovely touch. This sort of real charm is miles away from what Costner and Reynolds were after, and it shows.

Charm is a misunderstood commodity, however, and the critics came out like grave-diggers, leaving the field clear for Costner's film to sweep the board. As for Bergin, if you believed the *Monthly Film Bulletin* he turned out a 'well-mannered public schoolboy' – if you went along with *Empire* it was 'all bug-eyed stares and Oirish brogue from a fairly hopeless Bergin'.

13 A Downside to Fame

'You are only as good as your last picture,' Costner had admitted after *Dances with Wolves*, 'and mine happened to win seven Oscars, which was great, but how do you follow that?'

Increasingly, as it unfolded, *Robin Hood: Prince of Thieves* didn't seem to be the answer.

When filming wound up on the Morgan Creek production it was a heavy-hearted Reynolds that walked away from it. Throughout the experience he had clung to the advice Spielberg had once given him: 'Just survive it'. In fact, it was now that Reynolds needed that sense of survival more than ever, for he was kept away from the completion of the movie, as was his editor, Peter Boyle, though Morgan Creek, under the conditions of the Directors Guild, was obliged to show Reynolds a completed cut of what they had done to his original movie. He wasn't impressed.

'I thought a lot of what they'd done was pretty embarrassing, so I told them so, and they did what they wanted after that.'

One of the main thrusts of the producers' interference was cutting out much of Rickman's Sheriff and replacing him with Costner's Hood. Worryingly for the film's makers, test viewings in America disclosed the fact that audiences found Rickman more interesting than Costner. Reynolds was allowed no hand in the final cutting and mixing of the movie, and had to stand by helpless (if a good deal richer) as Morgan Creek dished up a picture that, said Reynolds, should have been shorter and sharper.

But the deepest cut was the rift in his relationship with his leading man. Reynolds felt, not without some justification, that Costner had turned his back on him and played ball with the producers. Ultimately, he had sanctioned the removal of Reynolds from the creative process, and allowed the director's work to be pulled apart. To Reynolds it must have seemed a betrayal, and the camaraderie they enjoyed could never be the same again.

'I have to say our friendship's not what it once was,' said Reynolds. 'It was a painful and disappointing process and I'm really sorry we're not as close as we were. You'd think that someone that's a friend would respect you enough as a film-maker to not try to interfere with what you're trying to do. I haven't talked to him for several months.'

When the final version of *Prince of Thieves* was issued, Reynolds went into a cinema to see it, but couldn't sit through more than the first couple of reels. He had wanted 'the chance to cross the line of making something realistic – and take that occasional fantastic step. I am also trying to expand the boundaries of each character, because I hate one-dimensional movies.'

What audiences discovered was a Robin returning to England from the third of Richard the Lionheart's crusades against the infidel Turk, allowing Reynolds a bloodthirsty and violent opening scene in the Holy Land's death cells, which made the film look as if it was going to be a remake of *The Count of Monte Cristo*. Robin teams up and escapes with the Moor, Azeem (Freeman), and together they sail for England, but Robin's homecoming is soured by the news that his father (Brian Blessed in the briefest of cameos) has been murdered. The quaking old family retainer Duncan (Walter Sparrow) tells his young master this was the work of the sheriff of Nottingham (Rickham), who has also gouged out Duncan's eyes.

Our hero introduces Azeem to his homeland *en route* to meeting Maid Marian (Mastrantonio). A masked figure who attacks him and kicks him in the crotch is revealed as

Hoping that seeing is believing in the magical *Field of Dreams*
are, *left to right* Gaby Hoffman, Costner and Amy Madigan

Costner cradling the dying Madeleine Stowe in *Revenge*, one of
the few affecting moments in a relentlessly violent movie

Costner, Madeleine Stowe and Anthony Quinn in a memento of *Revenge*. It was a pity that three such powerfully attractive actors should be mixed up in this mélange of excess and pointlessness

The white man carries Stands with a Fist (Mary McDonnell) back to her people in *Dances with Wolves*

Costner, as a deeply troubled guardian of America's doubts, listens to some home truths from Donald Sutherland in *JFK*

John Dunbar riding out for America, before he became a Sioux
called Dances with Wolves

Marian – an absurdity, as Marian could never have come up with the brute force of the masked attacker. But the attraction between Robin and Marian is obvious. Robin, with Azeem, enters Sherwood Forest where, after an amusing river-fight with John Little (Nick Brimble), Robin is feared drowned. Showing his mettle, Robin is accepted by the drop-outs of the wood, making their lives secure from the evil influences of the world beyond, though young Will Scarlett (Slater) has his doubts about the new arrival. His lack of feeling for Robin is transformed when he discovers he is Robin's half-brother.

The sheriff's desire to bed Marian, and his countless awful deeds, make him the sworn enemy of Robin. The Church and the blackly-magical crone Mortianna (McEwan, telling the future with the help of blood and sputum) team up with Nottingham against good Robin, but he organizes and inspires the rabble of Sherwood Forest and becomes their leader. When the sheriff's black-hearted cousin Guy of Gisborne (Michael Wincott) fails to stop Robin's progress, the sheriff embraces him comfortingly and drives a sword through him.

'Cancel the kitchen scraps for lepers and orphans,' dictates the sheriff. 'No more merciful beheadings, and call off Christmas.'

Inevitably, after Marian has told the much-travelled Robin to take a bath, she comes across him taking it in the nude by a waterfall (an idea more effectively used in *A Room with a View*). The tranquillity of life in the forest, and the birth of Little John's child (made safe by the skills of the misunderstood Azeem) provide some of the best things in the movie, but the serenity is soon shattered when Nottingham's men lay the plantation bare. Robin leads his men against the corrupt rulers, and is just in time to prevent the sheriff from raping Marian (hastily undergoing a marriage service carried out by Harold Innocent's delightfully sleazy bishop). Robin despatches the sheriff, who enjoys a nicely protracted death scene. The world is suddenly a better place, at least around Nottingham. Richard the Lionheart looks in to offer his congratulations, and Robin and Marian are free to marry.

The main question is, what sort of film would this have

been if Kevin Reynolds had been allowed to direct it the way he wanted? It looks handsome enough, has a rousing score (not in the same league as that by Korngold for the Flynn) and some exciting and heart-stopping moments, mostly thanks to some good photography and Reynolds' fast-moving, often swooping, style of shooting. But what of the rest?

The screenplay is the basis of all, and this is feeble stuff. Costner can do little with his lines, and we share no great belief in his convictions. He looks too heavy for the role, too – this is not the slim figure of *The Untouchables* or *Field of Dreams*. Costner may make for a less spectacular, more real Robin, than Fairbanks or Flynn, but he altogether lacks their sense of dare-devilling, of cheekiness, of pert and easy-come sexiness. We are asked to accept, in their place, another nude scene from Costner, this time posing at the waterfall, giving us the chance of another examination of what we had already seen in *Dances with Wolves*. Some felt this generous displaying of himself was getting to be something of a trademark.

It is left to Rickman to give a petulant, animal edge to the picture with his comic-book villainy, even though Rickman's playing, smouldering with black lust, belongs in a totally different movie. Rickman is more entertaining than Costner (as, in pantomime, King Rat has rather more going for him than the Good Fairy who thwarts him) but the humour here is so leaden, overdone and witless as to beggar belief. Worse, somewhere amongst all this camp intrusion, the core of Robin Hood's story, and crucial themes, such as Robin's manifesto of stealing from the rich to give to the poor, are lost. This is an aspect that could surely have been successfully exploited in a world gripped by recession; the Flynn version had managed to do so, subtly, coming out as it did during some of America's darkest days.

But this is a movie that goes for the simplest option at every turn. When there is an easy laugh available – usually a kick in the groin – we have to have it. And, for a movie that sells itself on being ideal family entertainment, it's a little crass to have a comic baddy who burns out old men's eyes, hangs children and rapes women. Such farcical elements need very careful handling, and they get none here.

In Sherwood, the Merrie Men are a dull lot. Christian Slater, barely justifying third billing, is a slight and uncomplicated Will Scarlett, though his American twang at least lets Costner feel less lonely. Friar Tuck is fat but otherwise unappealing, and one carries away only dim recollections of the others. It is left to a few supporting players – Innocent, Wincott and McEwan – to give the best of themselves, until the closing moments when Connery's sudden appearance never failed to bring the one spontaneous cheer of the evening from the audience. Some of their huge pleasure at seeing him may have been because they viewed Connery as a valued friend, some through sheer relief that, at the end of a long haul, an actor strolled into view who seemed to have the measure of what he was doing.

If the price of Costner and Reynolds' friendship seemed a small one to the producers, perhaps the public reaction to the movie justified their hard-headedness. Within ten days of its American opening on 14 June 1991 the movie had taken $45 million, and by February 1992 over $160 million. In Britain, where it premiered on 19 July 1991, it was a colossal success, playing all over the country well into the autumn. The people who bought tickets obviously adored it, which was good enough news for James Robinson.

'Word of mouth is what makes a film a big hit, not the critics,' he suggested. 'Remember *Ghost* got tepid reviews? *Prince of Thieves* is getting excellent word-of-mouth recommendation. When we previewed it, it scored 92 out of 100. Audiences loved it.'

The movie certainly had something going for it that even those who disliked it could praise: its brilliant trailer. If Costner was impressed by it, anyone could be.

'Have you seen the trailer?' he enthused. 'The trailer's fantastic. When I look at it, I've actually got to go see this movie. I don't want to say it crosses every demographic line, but *Robin Hood* has gone from being very uncool to very cool.'

Tactfully, Robinson had overlooked what another

bunch of people – the critics – had to say, which was a long way from the idolatry he would have liked to hear. The guarantee that Costner's name on the marquee seemed to give the movie did not prevent a good deal of bad feeling from the American press, that had some people suggesting there might be a sort of orchestrated backlash against Costner. Certainly, the complaints were laid thick across newspaper columns.

The *New Yorker* found *Prince of Thieves* 'a dull, dutiful trek … Watching this picture is about as much fun as paying taxes, and far less stirring emotionally. We never feel that anyone involved had any real affection for the story … there's not much joy in evidence here. Kevin Costner seems miscast as Robin: he's not a forceful enough actor for this role'. For the *New York Post* it was 'so politically correct it isn't any fun'. Vincent Canby in the *New York Times* found it 'a mess, a big, long, joyless reconstruction of the legend'.

Neither was the British press impressed with what Costner, Reynolds, and whoever it may have concerned at Morgan Creek, had done with dependable Robin. 'This latest incarnation of the legend is considerably smaller than the sum of its parts', wrote Philip Thomas in *Empire*; 'nearly everything that happened has been done before, and better, in movies from *Beetlejuice* to *Die Hard*'. Thomas went on to write of Costner 'frankly sleep-walking' through his part. The *Daily Telegraph* tackled the film's pretentiousness as it 'campaigns against all the modish sins which so excite the American campus', while, for the *Sunday Times*, George Perry noted that the 'generally humourless Costner … applies himself to the task with the same doggedness with which he faced the wilderness in *Dances with Wolves*. He has a dull and earnest speaking manner which tends to become monotonous … Costner is not much good in the romantic scenes.'

'If I could go back, I wouldn't make the movie again,' said Costner. 'Not because it's not any good, but because environment is important to me. So I've learned some lessons, yes, but that doesn't mean I won't make the same mistakes again.'

Costner's trip to Britain to film *Robin Hood* did not, on

any level, turn out a very happy experience. When details of his visit to a London nightclub, Stringfellows, burst into print in the tabloid press in late February 1991, he had fallen victim of his own success as well as of reporters scratching around for a celebrity scandal.

The girl in question was one Sheri Stewart, who claimed she had been picked up by Costner at the club and invited back to his hotel, where his love-making ('He was a wolf in my bed,' she promised) had kept her busy until eight o'clock the next morning. His attentions, she assured journalists, had brought tears to her eyes. What is more, Costner obviously had a fondness for the girl, as he saw her more than once. She was surprised to see a photograph of Cindy, discovering that she bore a close resemblance to her.

At about the same time, Cindy herself was bringing the children to London to see their father. Meanwhile, Costner took his girlfriend to a private screening of his latest movie, on which occasion Ms Stewart felt jealous of the girls involved with him on the screen. The relationship between Costner and Sheri Stewart came to an end when one of Costner's friends telephoned her to tell her it was over. Having done the public the service of exposing Costner's antics to their notice, Sheri assumed outrage when shown some old cuttings of Costner's adolescent talk about women, of the days when he had, no doubt with a disarming naïvety, referred to them as 'sluts'.

'I'm no slut,' protested Sheri, 'but he certainly treated me like one. He was only interested in me as a sex object, and not as a woman. My impression of him was of a carefree bachelor about town – not a happily married man with three kids. But I'm a grown woman, and the chemistry was right between us, so I stayed put. And he was great in bed.'

Her parting gambit that 'any man who uses the word slut as a term of endearment has got to have problems,' closed the matter – at least for Sheri. Costner had his own feelings about the way the story had been written up by the British press.

'They were off the wall. Maybe I'd think about these things differently if I didn't have a family that can be hurt.

My wife and I have had to learn, after sixteen years, how to handle this new situation ... There's a big strain on us of just how much publicity will come with success. It's a strain we haven't dealt with before. Let's face it, the public can only take this good guy story about me for just so long. It's wearing thin.'

For the prince of Britain's gossip columnists, Nigel Dempster, there was no doubt that there were girls in London who made it their business to work themselves into the lives of the rich and famous and then spill their stories to Fleet Street.

'They are looking for people like Kevin Costner. But in no circumstances was he on the loose, procuring women, constantly randy.'

Nevertheless, news of Hollywood's most happily married male star, the actor who for years had trumpeted his devotion to wife and family, and tried to hold himself up as an example of clean-living America, was going to interest a lot of people. Fox Television wasted no time in interviewing Sheri Stewart in London; obligingly, she gave them a straight-down-the-line account of her evening with, if she was to be believed, this predatory Lothario. Fox made the interview available to its New York office, who wasted no time in arranging transmission of the kiss-and-tell account coast-to-coast.

Then, as suddenly as it had been scheduled, the interview was shelved, through the intervention of the agent Costner had left J.J. Harris for – Michael Ovitz. Ovitz, wielding the considerable power of Hollywood's most influential actors' agency, CAA, had called Fox's office. Perhaps it was no coincidence that the Academy Awards, with Kevin Costner and *Dances with Wolves* writ large, was only one week away – the loss of *gravitas* to the Costner image would have been, to put it mildly, undesirable.

By the time Sheri Stewart's story hit the headlines, the source of her romantic anxiety was safely back home, where he and Cindy were variously reported – not surprisingly – as thrashing out ways of stabilizing their marriage. Meanwhile, his expected reappearance in Britain as the subject of a *Guardian* lecture at the National

Film Theatre in February 1991 did not materialize; Costner gave the Gulf War as his reason for cancelling his presence.

But 1991 persisted in looking like Costner's year of embarrassment when another reared its head, this time perpetuated on film, when *Truth or Dare* (called *In Bed with Madonna* in Britain) opened across America. By default, Costner found himself a bit player in a fly-on-the-wall movie about superstar Madonna. Its director, Alek Keshishian, had filmed over 248 hours of the singer-actress both on- and off-stage, which itself qualified him for an Academy Award for endurance. From this unending flow of Madonna he had selected what he, presumably, thought were the most fascinating moments.

The movie told audiences little about Madonna they hadn't already guessed, and certainly proved her personality wasn't what you would call lovable. There was at least some educational value, as when we watched Madonna's unique method of picking petals from a flower to discover her true love ('He loves me ... he loves me not ... he wants to fuck me ... '). There were also some telling moments when she was shown escorted by Warren Beatty, an unhappy smile fixed to his face and awaiting her command: 'You pussy man, get over here.'

Costner, too, had managed to get involved in this imbroglio when he made a spontaneous backstage visit to Madonna after one of her concerts. Looking decidedly fuller in the face than he had in *Dances with Wolves*, Costner embarrassingly greeted the singer, told her how much he had appreciated the show, and described it as 'Neat'. Her reception, of the type known as cool, obviously had Costner wishing this was one backstage call he hadn't made. He blew a perfunctory kiss to her, and left. Turning away, Madonna put her fingers down her throat in a gagging mime.

'Neat?' she snarls quietly. 'Anybody who says my show is neat has to go.'

On this evidence, it seems unlikely that we shall ever have to sit through a movie co-starring Kevin Costner and Madonna.

Less well publicized was a pathetic little incident that

showed Costner in an altogether different, and better, light. Among the many eagerly awaiting the release of Costner's latest movie was a terminally-ill 14-year-old boy. His one burning desire was to see *Robin Hood: Prince of Thieves*. With two weeks to go to its opening, doctors told his family the boy had only about a week to live. They succeeded in contacting Costner and telling him their story. Not only did Costner put on a special screening just for the boy, he also sat beside him throughout, and gave him the leather pouch he had used in the movie.

14   Dealing with Camelot

Millions of people remember where they were, what they were doing, when the news came through that John F. Kennedy, 35th President of the United States, had been assassinated as his motor cavalcade drove along Dealey Plaza in Dallas, Texas. The date was 22 November 1963.

A 17-year-old high school student, Oliver Stone, was taking a lunch break when he heard. 'I didn't realize my life had changed forever,' he said later. An 8-year-old called Kevin Costner was sent home with the rest of his third grade class after his mother had called on the principal with the news of Kennedy's death. It didn't seem like something that would have a devastating effect on America's consciousness, but as both boys grew to manhood the tremendous implications of what had happened became increasingly apparent. In late November 1963, however, there seemed to be an almost indecent haste to tie up the facts surrounding the President's death in one big, neat bow. The solution to 'Who Killed Kennedy?' was offered as something simplistic and easily assimilated, shutting the lid on a Pandora's box of doubt, theory and supposition.

What America, having hardly recovered from the shock of seeing their leader's murder relayed by television into their homes, was given to understand, was straightforward. John F. Kennedy had been shot by a man called Lee Harvey Oswald, a one-time US marine and active Communist, from the sixth floor of the Texas School Book Depository. Oswald had also shot and killed a policeman who had tried to apprehend him. Arraigned before the television cameras, Oswald protested his innocence, saying he was 'the patsy' of the whole affair. Two days after Kennedy's death, Oswald was shot dead by a night-club owner, Jack Ruby. This second television-transmitted murder immediately created grave doubts as to whether the truth about the President's assassination would ever be known. Ruby was given a life sentence for the killing of Oswald, tried to kill himself in prison, and died there in 1967 from a cancer that, he claimed, had been induced by his captors.

Eight months after the massacre at Dealey Plaza, Chief Justice Earl Warren's Presidential Commission issued a 26-volume report on the killing of the President, coming to the conclusion that Lee Harvey Oswald had, on his own and as part of no conspiracy, killed Kennedy. The Commission can hardly have expected their prosaic findings would satisfy all those who had been intrigued by the unanswered questions that plagued the issue. Among those nursing massive doubts about the official line was the District Attorney of New Orleans, Jim Garrison, who, to the embarrassment of the powers that be, now concocted his own theories that went far beyond the unexceptional pronouncements of Earl Warren.

It was in 1967 that Garrison had Clay Shaw, a high-living homosexual Texan businessman, brought to court on charges of conspiring to effect Kennedy's death. Garrison's case against him was eventually lost, though for Shaw the worst had been done. A broken man, he died four years later. Two years before Shaw's death, an investigating House Select Committee re-examined the evidence concerning the President's assassination and seemed to confirm much of what Garrison had been claiming. They decided that Kennedy's death had probably come about through some sort of conspiracy, though they would be drawn no further.

Ten years later, Garrison poured his theories into a fascinating book, *On the Trail of the Assassins*, its gung-ho title evoking the spirit of a game of cowboys and Indians. The implications of this extraordinary story being made into a film were enormous, and could have been no more dangerous than in the hands of the director who secured the rights – Oliver Stone.

Stone's relationship with the US government and establishment has always been contentious, and in *JFK* (as Stone's movie was to be called) the contention was white-hot. A paranoia of distrust and hatred was whipped up long before the picture was released, as Stone's destructive way with his country's pronounced morals and political stance reared its unwelcome head again. Why should anyone have been surprised to find America holding its hands up in horror at the idea of Stone making his inevitably personal comment on an event that had ripped out the heart of his country?

The director responsible for such painfully questioning movies as *Salvador* (America's doings in Central America), *Platoon* (America's doings in Vietnam), *Wall Street* (America's fashionable acquisitiveness), and *Born on the Fourth of July* (America's attitude to its war veterans), could hardly have expected the establishment to welcome any film bearing his name. If Stone's disturbing discontent with America's recent history was to get its hands on the assassination of John F. Kennedy, the floodgates of recklessness, inaccuracy and prejudice would – according to Stone's critics – be opened wide. An ageing Pauline Kael rather maliciously explained that one of the main reasons she had retired as a film critic was so that never again would she have to sit through another Oliver Stone movie.

From the moment filming began in March 1991, sometimes on location at the very spot where the events of the fateful day had unfolded, Stone and his film became the focal point of America's censure. In May 1991 an article entitled 'Dallas in Wonderland' appeared in the *Washington Post*, making a pitiless attack on the movie's script, and painting Stone as an evil public enemy. He was pictured in a monstrous cartoon as America's very own Saddam Hussein. In the same journal, Harold Weisberg said of Stone, 'I think people who sell sex have more principle.'

The Warren Commission's chief investigator denounced *JFK* as 'a big lie which would make Adolf Hitler proud'. A fellow-member of the Commission, ex-President Gerald Ford, dismissed Stone's work as a 'desecration of the memory of President Kennedy and a fraudulent misrepresentation of the truth'. To make matters worse, a potential *Robin Hood: Prince of Thieves* fiasco seemed to be on the horizon, with news that another movie about Kennedy's assassination was slated for production, based on Don DeLillo's novel *Oswald*. The film company wanting to get it started joined in the *JFK* slanging match, accusing Stone of intimidation, and of attempting to keep their movie on the back-burner.

For Kevin Costner to have become involved in a project as politically fraught as *JFK* may be seen by some as no more than the next step along a natural progression. The journey, after all, had been a long one. In *Fandango*, he had been all that was misunderstood, but basically thoroughly good, about American adolescence; in *Silverado*, the wind had been in his hair as he looked out on how America should always have been – wide, open, free; in *The Untouchables*, he hadn't minced his words or beliefs, letting everyone know he was there to do some good deeds in a dark world ... and so Costner's screen persona had developed. More recently, he had added to these achievements with the politically correct, antiseptic goodness he pushed forward both in *Dances with Wolves* and *Robin Hood: Prince of Thieves*.

Perhaps surprisingly, Costner didn't respond well to the idea of playing Garrison when Oliver Stone brought the screenplay to England for the actor to consider during the making of *Robin Hood*. To begin with, he was exhausted after the rigours of *Dances with Wolves*, from which he had straightaway plunged into the maelstrom of *Robin Hood*, with no time to collect himself. He felt Cindy and the children were owed some time, a vacation of two or three months, away from all the pressures of his career. If it had been left to Costner, he would almost certainly have turned Stone down, but Cindy picked up on the idea, looked at the script and told him he should do it, as much for the sake of his country as for himself. It seemed a strange decision for a die-hard supporter of George Bush to come up with, but Costner had an explanation.

'People don't really know what my political persuasion is – they think they do and they editorialize what I might be, but it's not all I am. I am a Bush supporter, but I'm not in complete agreement with everything that's going on with that situation.'

Coming to terms with his political stance on the issues he would have to deal with on screen, Costner signed up with Stone for a $7 million fee, plus a slice of the movie's profits. By the time the film appeared, he was asking journalists to make it absolutely clear that, though Bush was a close friend of his, the President had not questioned Costner's involvement with *JFK*, though Mr Bush can hardly not have wondered how Costner's fiercely Republican ticket could have taken him so far beyond the pale as to make so poisonous a political statement with the ever-unwelcome Oliver Stone. Taking a break during filming, Costner went off to the White House to play a companionable 18 holes of golf with his President-friend, during which, presumably, the nature of Costner's current venture was tactfully avoided.

'In Los Angeles the charge has been levelled at me that I'm politically correct,' said Costner. 'I would like to take issue with that because to be 'politically correct' in Hollywood is to be really liberal ... we have huge cracks in this country that have to be addressed and I don't think such issues are either Republican or Democratic. I think they're humanitarian.'

With Pauline Kael leading the band of anti-Costner critics by declaring *Dances with Wolves* to be no more than 'simple-minded mush', and the shoals of bad notices that had come as such a shock in the wake of *Robin Hood*, there was a danger that, nowadays, any statement from Kevin Costner sounded a little portentous, a little self-important. There seemed to be no reluctance in him to face up to pointing out America's bad ways. He seemed to suggest that it could try harder and do better through the magic potency of the messages proclaimed in his movies. 'I'm in love with my country,' said Costner. 'I do know that the clear, philosophical voice we had with Kennedy is gone. We need to have a philosophical stance in this world.'

Quite what Costner's understanding of the facts

surrounding Kennedy's death is is not quite clear, for he made it known that while he accepted Garrison's general argument that Lee Harvey Oswald had not acted by himself and that a conspiracy had gone undetected by the Warren Commission, he by no means saw eye to eye with everything Stone put into the mouths of his characters.

And here lies the crucial problem with *JFK* – not that Stone had dramatized what Garrison had written, or the facts and theories presented in the movie's other source book, Jim Marrs' *Crossfire: The Plot that Killed Kennedy*, or the ideas worked up by the gaggle of other researchers beavering away behind *JFK*, but that he had fictionalized the truth, and so distorted the argument that it was no longer possible to differentiate truth from fiction. Stone tended to wave such criticism aside, defending his film as a 'hypothesis, based on fact'. This is all very well when you are dealing with Cornel Wilde in a weepy biopic of Chopin, but spicing up the events behind the assassination of one of America's most legendary, but actual figures is surely another matter.

What is perhaps equally unacceptable is that we are presented with the story in such very black and white terms. In fact, the distinction Stone makes between good and evil even recalls the uncomplicated distinction between what is nice and what is nasty in *The Untouchables*, for Stone doesn't bother with anything more than primary colours when it comes to characterization. Garrison at home, as played by Costner, is so comfy, slippers-by-the-fire content, surrounded by his supportive wife (Sissy Spacek wasting away in a boring role), stipulated sweet children, and lumbering family pet, that he is no more than a rerun of dull old Eliot Ness. These home-loving scenes of *JFK* are pretty hard to swallow, accentuating Garrison's goodness to almost farcical proportions.

As for evil, it is here so diametrically opposed to good that we need no deeper understanding of it, as with Stone's depiction of Shaw's homosexual activities. The problem here is that, even if we accept Stone's depressingly sordid account of gay life, most of what we are given is a complete fabrication. The muscular, ratty little rent-boy (beautifully played by Kevin Bacon) is a complete fiction, here made to add potency to Stone's theorizing. Perhaps, at least, the last laugh is with the gay element, which also has the advantage of a terrific performance from Tommy Lee Jones as Shaw and Joe Pesci as the sadly-toupeed David Ferrie, for Stone can't make his straight characters anywhere near as interesting.

What Stone and Costner have also done in *JFK* is to perpetuate the unquestioned idolatry of a President whose public face of princely young statesmanship often belied the man behind it. Of personal criticism directed at the President, *JFK* has very little (one or two dissenting voices early on, and, of course, the venom of the conspirators which actually amounts to nothing). Elsewhere, he is somehow perceived as a fount of wisdom and collective decency, making him the ideal by which Americans can measure themselves. Never mind that he was, throughout his short life, a very sick man, suffering from Addison's disease, given to fits of collapse, needing daily jabs of cortisone. At low moments in his history, the Last Rites had twice been administered.

He didn't want 18-year-olds to get the vote, and made a personal plea to Martin Luther King, asking him to call off his planned civil rights march on Washington (that had given birth to King's world-inspiring speech). On the home front, his relationship with Congress was troubled, bill after bill being sent back to the White House. The man credited with all the right values also had what appeared to be a perfect marriage to the svelte Jacqueline. It was a façade. Besides his affair with Marilyn Monroe, there were to be countless assignations with women. One writer described him as 'compulsive as Mussolini – up against the wall, Signora, if you have five minutes', another said he hadn't finished with a girl until he'd had her three ways.

But such a character assessment of the President never finds its way into *JFK*. What Stone and Costner seem content to do is accept the fact that Kennedy was the best thing that had happened to America for years; it is the bedrock of a movie that never begins to question its basic premise. The murky goings-on around the event of his death are nevertheless fascinatingly presented, even if there is the dangerous quality of not being able to tell real-life footage from acted scenes.

Some critics have seen the movie as an attempt to show American society as riddled by corruption, but this is surely a total misunderstanding of what *JFK* is about. It may have an excess of villains (so does *Batman*) but, when the chips are down, it is our hero that alone matters, our hero who stands for all the things we like to think we stand for and believe in.

This is obvious at the end of the movie, a long set piece for Costner, laying out his ideals in the courtroom via an impassioned tirade. The words and sentiments may well be as much those of Oliver Stone and Kevin Costner as Jim Garrison but we can at last anchor our trust to our hero – recalling, as Costner could hardly help recalling, James Stewart's peroration at the end of *Mr Smith Goes to Washington*. The integrity Costner was able to demonstrate here is evidence enough of the extraordinary maturity he has grown into in only a few years at the top of his profession. Now, looking ahead, his future was at once made and uncertain. Professionally, *Dances with Wolves* and *JFK* placed him at the peak of his craft, and beyond him the old tightrope of success stretched out. Personally, there were many problems to contend with, as Jim Wilson confirmed.

'Fame has forced Kevin to reassess a lot of stuff. There's a great deal more available to him in every way. He can make changes and impact a large population. Suddenly, he has this loaded gun, where ten years ago he didn't.'

It was Stone who took most of the flak when it was handed out on the film's release, Costner's attempt to somewhat distance himself from the politics of the movie apparently having worked. Iain Johnstone in the *Sunday Times* said that the Garrison shown on screen was not the real, everyday Garrison but 'Saint James … as played (quite excellently) by Kevin Costner, a golden aura of honesty and patriotic purity surrounds the lawman, as if transferred from the dead president himself … [the film is] a supreme act of propaganda … a script that combines pride and prejudice in equal measure'. Henry Sheenan in

Sight and Sound thought that 'Kevin Costner plays Garrison, as he plays practically every other character from Eliot Ness to Robin Hood, as a dignified loner going his own way ...'

As film-making, *JFK* is a superbly crafted piece of work, but as a document that will be handed down as, at least, a version of what caused the killing of President John F. Kennedy, it could not be more contentious. It is all very well for Stone and Costner to point out the speculative nature of the screenplay, and the liberal treatment of known facts, but who is to explain all this to future generations sitting down to watch it? Perhaps, ultimately, none of this matters, for Costner (with Stone's permission) had once again, as he had in *Dances with Wolves*, rewritten history into a neat package, charged it through with high emotion, and presented it as a sort of beacon signing the path America should take.

Politics, of course, is something Costner has tried, so often, to brush aside, dodging the accusations that his off-screen beliefs don't exactly match up with his on-screen posings. In distancing himself from all this, there is still the suspicion that, in the future, politics may come to have a much greater role to play in his career. There are those who recognized, in his performance as Garrison, a tendency to play Garrison as if he were the President himself – and certainly upholding the standards Kennedy had seemed to set forth. If Costner's real-life beliefs match up to his screen image, the White House might want for no better tenant.

Meanwhile, there is the unenviable occupation of being the leading thirtysomething in Hollywood. A.P. Herbert knew a thing or two about the human condition, and Costner would probably agree with one of the phrases Herbert passed into the English language – 'It's tough at the top'. From the nowhere of the early eighties, Costner has emerged, in a brief run of movies, as top of the heap. At the Hollywood top, success absolutely guarantees he won't be waiting in line for bread, but the stardom comes complete with its own furniture of fear, doubt, and – perhaps worst of all – restriction. This is bad news for the creative spirit. Chances that the young, untried Costner might have taken (and did take) would be very much more difficult to take on now he is a mature, successful star.

Next up for him is a movie with Whitney Houston – *The Bodyguard* – about which there will be an aura of huge expectancy, for Miss Houston's acting debut as much as for Costner's participation. He has also said he wants to play Arthur in Lerner and Loewe's *Camelot*, perhaps hoping to live out a fantasy of the original Camelot in an attempt to forget the hideous collapse of his country's own dream of freedom and peace. And, though European audiences have not had the chance to hear the recordings he has made, it seems that Costner can sing. At this time, his singing career, restricted to some pop material put out in safely far-distant countries, hasn't threatened to take over his work in movies.

The problems facing Costner as a film actor are, of course, very different from those that faced the actors he has so often been compared with – James Stewart, Gary Cooper, or whoever. They lived through the Golden Age of Hollywood, ruled by the studio system, passing from one movie to another, often making several a year. Sometimes, they had scant idea of exactly what the movie they were setting out on was all about. That was then. Costner is, of course, not the first actor to take his own career by the scruff of the neck and pursue it along his own lines. Continuing success has ensured that he can do so, and, with only an occasional blip here and there (*Revenge* being probably the noisiest), Costner has established a unique place in contemporary popular cinema.

'Popular' may, indeed, be the key word, for Costner's career rides on movies that apparently carry meaningful messages but remain totally accessible. Increasingly, there is the feeling that Costner's audiences and his critics – once in agreement about his qualities and worthiness – are parting company. This will probably have very little effect on his future.

The real man – happily, steadfastly married to his college sweetheart, with his three children, his fiercely-guarded privacy, his reputation as nothing more or less than 'one of the boys' – will carry on being matched to his on-screen image.

He himself was pleased to be compared to Steve McQueen. He liked the no-nonsense feel about that, for Costner is a man who looks comfortable with other men. He looks good among them. He looks very good among women. He looks good holding a gun. He looks good wearing clothes and looks good without them. But none of this is good enough for Costner himself, none of it seems to satisfy him enough. He wants to make movies that mean something, that contribute to the argument of life.

It may be mere coincidence that, of all his movies, the three that seem to offer some sort of message most heavily – *Dances with Wolves, Robin Hood: Prince of Thieves* and *JFK* – are those that have been the more attacked by his critics. And Costner can look at the success of all three and feel happy that his audiences, by and large, swallowed them whole.

Other books will, of course, be written about Kevin Costner. Taking into consideration twenty, thirty, forty years of his life and career will lead other writers into very different assessments. They may very well take a grandiose view and applaud a lifetime's achievement at the feet of ... inevitably, James Stewart, Gary Cooper ... or any of the heroes of Hollywood, holding up a mirror to show a reflection of what their country wants to see. The fact that Costner increasingly seems intent on showing his country what it does not want to see makes the comparison all the more interesting.

For his own part, Costner may well go through life protesting he's just an ordinary guy. For all we know, he may be right. What has happened to Kevin Costner had, after all, to happen to somebody.

Bibliography

Agan, Patrick, *Robert De Niro: The man, the myth and the movies* (Robert Hale, 1989)

Blake, Michael, *Dances with Wolves* (US, Ballantine Books, 1988)

Brode, Douglas, *The Films of the Eighties* (US, Citadel, 1990)

Buscombe, Edward, (ed), *The British Film Institute Companion to the Western* (Deutsch, 1988)

Costner, Kevin, et al., *Dances with Wolves* (US, Newmarket Press, 1990)

Ebert, Roger, *Movie Home Companion* (US, Andrews and McMeel, 1991)

Garrison, Jim, *On the Trail of the Assassins* (US, Sheridan Square Press, 1988)

Grobel, Lawrence, *The Hustons* (Bloomsbury, 1990)

Kael, Pauline, *Hooked: Film writings 1985–1988* (Marion Boyars, 1990)

Keith, Todd, *Kevin Costner* (Ikonprint, 1991)

Milne, Tom, (ed.), *The Time Out Film Guide*: Second edition (Penguin, 1991)

The Motion Picture Annual (US, Cinebooks, various editions)

Park, James, (ed.), *The Virgin Film Yearbook* (Virgin, various editions)

Pearce, Garth, *Robin Hood: Prince of Thieves* (Hamlyn, 1991)

Pickard, Roy, *Who Played Who on Screen* (Batsford, 1988)

Shipman, David, *The Great Movie Stars 3: The independent years* (Macdonald, 1991)

Filmography

SIZZLE BEACH (aka SIZZLE BEACH USA and MALIBU HOT SUMMER) 1974

Director: Richard Brander

SHADOWS RUN BLACK
Mesa Films/Media Gallery. 1981 (released 1983). 89 minutes.

Director: Howard Heard. Producer: Eric Louzil. Screenplay: Craig Kusaba, Duke Howard. Photography: John Sprung. Editors: Paul Davalos, Davide Ganzino. Music: Steve Mann.

Leading Players: Elizabeth Trosper (Judy Cole), William J. Kulzer (Rydell King), Shea Porter (Morgan Cole), George J. Engelson (Priest), Dianne Hinkler (Helen Cole), Julius Metoyer (Billy Tovar), Terry Congie (Lee Faulkner), Lee Bishop (Police Officer).
Kevin Costner plays the role of Jimmy Scott, but currently available prints do not contain any credit of his performance.

CHASING DREAMS
Nascent. 1981 (released 1989). 94 minutes.

Directors: Sean Roche, Therese Conte. Producers: David G. Brown, Therese Conte, Marc Schwartz. Screenplay:

David G. Brown. Photography: Connie Holt. Editors: Jerry Weldon, Robert Sinise. Design: Bobbi Peterson Himber. Music: Gregory Conte.

Leading Players: David G. Brown (Gavin), John Fife (Parks), Jim Shane (Father), Matthew Clark (Ben), Lisa Kingston (Sue), Claudia Carroll (Mother).
    Other players include: Cecilia Bennett, Kelly McCarthy, Don Margolin, Marc Brandes, Dan Waldman and Kevin Costner.

FRANCES
Brooksfilms. 1982. 140 minutes.

Director: Graeme Clifford. Producer: Jonathan Sanger. Screenplay: Eric Bergren, Christopher Devore, Nicholas Kazan. Photography: Laszlo Kovacs. Design: Richard Sylbert. Editor: John Wright. Music: John Barry.

Leading Players: Jessica Lange (Frances Farmer), Sam Shepard (Harry York), Kim Stanley (Lillian Farmer), Bart Burns (Ernest Farmer), Lane Smith (Dr Symington), Allan Rich (Mr Beebe), Jeffrey DeMunn (Clifford Odets), Sarah Cunningham (Alma Styles), Donald Craig (Ralph Edwards), Christopher Pennock (Dick Steele), Gerald O'Loughlin (Labotomy Doctor).
    Kevin Costner uncredited in two brief scenes.

NIGHT SHIFT
Warner Bros/Ladd (Brian Grazer). 1982. 106 minutes.

Director: Ron Howard. Producer: Brian Grazer. Screenplay: Lowell Ganz, Babaloo Mandel. Photography: James Crabe. Design: Jack Collis. Editors: Robert J. Kern, Daniel P. Hanley, Mike Hill. Music: Burt Bacharach.

Leading Players: Henry Winkler (Chuck Lumley), Michael Keaton (Bill Blaze Jowski), Shelley Long (Belinda Keaton), Gina Hecht (Charlotte Koogle), Pat Corley (Edward Koogle), Bobby DiCicco (Leonard), Nita Talbot (Vivian), Basil Hoffman (Drollhauser), Tim Rossovich (Luke), Clint

Howard (Jefferey), Joe Spinell (Manetti), Cheryl Carter (Tanya), Kevin Costner (Frat Boy 1).

STACY'S KNIGHTS (aka WINNING STREAK)
Crown International Pictures/American Twist. 1982. 94 minutes.

Director: Jim Wilson. Producers: Joann Locktov, Freddy Sweet. Screenplay: Michael Blake. Photography: Raul Lomas. Design: Florence Fellman. Editor: Bonnie Koehler. Music: Norton Buffalo.

Leading Players: Andra Millian (Stacy Lancaster), Kevin Costner (Will Bonner), Eve Lilith (Jean Dennison), Mike Reynolds (Shecky Poole), Garth Howard (Mr C), Ed Semenza (The Kid), Don Hackstaff (Lawyer), L. C. (Buster), Cheryl Ferris (Marion), Gary Tilles (Rudy), Roge Roush (Rollin), John Brevick (Floor Boss).

TABLE FOR FIVE
Voight-Schaffel Productions. 1983. 124 minutes.

Director: Robert Liberman. Producer: Robert Schaffel. Screenplay: David Seltzer. Photography: Vilmos Zsigmond. Design: Robert F. Boyle. Editor: Michael Kahn. Music: Miles Goodman, John Morris.

Leading Players: Jon Voight (J.P. Tanner), Richard Crenna (Mitchell), Marie Christine Barrault (Marie), Millie Perkins (Kathleen), Roxana Zal (Tilda), Bobby Kiger (Truman-Paul), Son Hoang Bui (Trung), Maria O'Brien (Mandy), Nelson Welch (Old Man), Kevin Costner (Newly-wed Husband), Cynthia Kania (Newly-wed Wife).

THE BIG CHILL
Columbia/Carson Productions (Michael Shamberg). 1983. 108 minutes.

Director: Lawrence Kasdan. Producer: Michael Shamberg. Screenplay: Lawrence Kasdan, Barbara Benedek. Photography: John Bailey. Design: Ida Random. Editor: Carol Littleton.

Leading Players: Tom Berenger (Sam), Glenn Close (Sarah), Jeff Goldblum (Michael), William Hurt (Nick), Kevin Kline (Harold), Mary Kay Place (Meg), Meg Tilly (Chloe), JoBeth Williams (Karen), Don Galloway (Richard), Kevin Costner (Alex).

TESTAMENT
Entertainment Events. 1983. 90 minutes.

Director: Lynne Littman. Producers: Jonathan Bernstein, Lynne Littman. Screenplay: John Sacret Young, based on the story *The Last Testament* by Carol Amen. Photography: Steven Poster. Editor: Suzanne Pettit. Music: James Horner.

Leading Players: Jane Alexander (Carol Wetherly), William Devane (Tom Wetherly), Ross Harris (Brad Wetherly), Roxana Zal (Mary Liz Wetherly), Lukas Haas (Scottie Wetherly), Philip Anglim (Hollis), Lilas Skala (Fania), Leon Ames (Henry Abhart), Lurene Tuttle (Rosemary Abhart), Rebecca De Mornay (Cathy Pitkin), Kevin Costner (Phil Pitkin).

THE GUNRUNNER
New World Pictures/Vision Voice. 1989. 79 minutes.

Director: Nardo Castillo. Producers: Richard Sadler, Robert J. Langevin. Screenplay: Arnie Gelbart. Photography: Alain Dostie. Design: Wendell Dennis. Editors: Diane Fingado, Andre Corriveau. Music: Rex Taylor Smith.

Leading Players: Kevin Costner (Ted Beaubien), Sara Botsford (Maude), Paul Soles (Lochman), Gerard Parkes (Wilson), Ron Lea (George), Mitch Martin (Rosalyn), Larry Lewis (Robert), Ruth Danan (Ada), Daniel Nalbach (Max), Martin Neufeld (Eddie), Pierre Thériault (Gabias), Sébastien Dhavernas (Fred Samuel).

FANDANGO
Warner Bros/Amblin Entertainment. 1984. 87 minutes.

Director: Kevin Reynolds. Producer: Tim Zinnemann. Screenplay: Kevin Reynolds. Photography: Thomas Del Ruth. Editor: Arthur Schmidt. Design: Peter Landsdown Smith. Music: Alan Silvestri.

Leading Players: Kevin Costner (Gardner Barnes), Judd Nelson (Phil Hicks), Sam Robards (Kenneth Waggener), Chuck Bush (Dorman), Brian Cesak (Lester), Elizabeth Daily (Judy), Suzy Amis (The Girl), Marvin J. McIntyre (Truman Sparks), Glenne Headly (Trelis), Pepe Serna (Gas Station Mechanic), Robyn Rose (Lorna).

AMERICAN FLYERS
WW/Warner Bros. 1985. 114 minutes.

Director: John Badham. Producers: Gareth Wigan, Paula Weinstein. Screenplay: Steve Tesich. Photography: Don Peterman. Editor: Frank Morriss. Design: Lawrence G. Paull. Music: Lee Ritenour, Greg Mathieson.

Leading Players: Kevin Costner (Marcus), David Grant (David), Rae Dawn Chong (Sarah), Alexandra Paul (Becky), Janice Rule (Mrs Sommers), Luca Bercovici (Muzzin), Robert Townsend (Jerome), John Amos (Dr Conrad), Doi Johnson (Randolph), John Garber (Belov), Jennifer Grey (Leslie).

SILVERADO
Columbia. 1985. 132 minutes.

Director/Producer: Lawrence Kasdan. Screenplay: Lawrence Kasdan, Mark Kasdan. Photography: John Bailey. Design: Ida Random. Editor: Carol Littleton. Music: Bruce Broughton.

Leading Players: Kevin Kline (Paden), Scott Glenn (Emmett), Rosanna Arquette (Hannah), John Cleese (Sheriff Langston), Kevin Costner (Jake), Brian Dennehy (Cobb), Danny Glover (Mal), Jeff Goldblum (Slick), Linda Hunt (Stella), Ray Baker (McKendrick), Joe Seneca (Ezra), Lynn Whitfield (Rae), Jeff Fahey (Tyree), Pepe Serna

(Scruffy), Patricia Gaul (Kate), Amanda Wyss (Phoebe), Earl Hindman (J.T.), James Gammon (Dawson), Tom Brown (Augie).

THE UNTOUCHABLES
 Paramount. 1987. 119 minutes.

Director: Brian De Palma. Producer: Art Linson. Screenplay: David Mamet. Photography: Stephen H. Burum. Design: William A. Elliott. Editors: Jerry Greenberg, Bill Pankow. Music: Ennio Morricone.

Leading Players: Kevin Costner (Eliot Ness), Sean Connery (Jim Malone), Charles Martin Smith (Oscar Wallace), Andy Garcia (George Stone), Robert De Niro (Al Capone), Richard Bradford (Mike), Jack Kehoe (Payne), Brad Sullivan (George), Billy Drago (Frank Nitti), Patricia Clarkson (Ness's Wife).

AMAZING STORIES
 Amblin Entertainment/Universal. 1987. 110 minutes.

(A portmanteau film comprising three screenplays: the second being MUMMY DADDY and the third GO TO THE HEAD OF THE CLASS. The first screenplay of the film, the only one featuring Costner, is THE MISSION, production details of which are given below.)

Director: Steven Spielberg. Producer: David E. Vogel. Screenplay: Menno Meyjes, from story by Steven Spielberg. Photography: John McPherson. Design: Rick Carter. Editor: Steven Kemper. Music: John Williams.

Leading Players: Kevin Costner (Captain Spark), Casey Siemaszko (Jonathan), Kiefer Sutherland (Static), Jeffrey Jay Cohen (Jake), John Philbin (Bullseye), Gary Mauro (Sam), Glen Mauro (Dave).

NO WAY OUT
 Orion. 1987. 115 minutes.

Director: Roger Donaldson. Producers: Laura Ziskin, Robert Garland. Screenplay: Robert Garland, based on the novel *The Big Clock* by Kenneth Fearing. Photography: John Alcott, Alun Bollinger. Design: Dennis Washington, Kai Hawkins. Editor: Neil Travis. Music: Maurice Jarre.

Leading Players: Kevin Costner (Tom Farrell), Gene Hackman (David Brice), Sean Young (Susan Atwell), Will Patton (Scott Pritchard), Howard Duff (Senator Duvall), George Dzundza (Sam Hesselman), Jason Bernard (Major Donovan), Iman (Nina Beka), Fred Dalton Thompson (Marshall), Leon Russom (Kevin O'Brien), Dennis Burkley (Mate).

BULL DURHAM
Mount Company/Orion. 1988. 108 minutes.

Director: Ron Shelton. Producers: Thom Mount, Mark Burg. Screenplay: Ron Shelton. Photography: Bobby Byrne. Design: Armin Ganz. Editors: Robert Leighton, Adam Weiss. Music: Michael Convertino.

Leading Players: Kevin Costner (Crash Davis), Susan Sarandon (Annie Savoy), Tim Robbins (Ebby Calvin 'Nuke' LaLoosh), Trey Wilson (Joe 'Skip' Riggins), Robert Wuhl (Larry Hockett), William O'Leary (Jimmy), David Neidorf (Bobby), Danny Gans (Deke), Tom Silardi (Tony), Jenny Robertson (Millie), Rick Marzan (Jose), George Buck (Nuke's Father), Lloyd Williams (Mickey), Max Patkin 'The Clown Prince of Baseball' as himself.

FIELD OF DREAMS
Gordon Company/Universal. 1989. 106 minutes.

Director: Phil Alden Robinson. Producers: Lawrence Gordon, Charles Gordon. Screenplay: Phil Alden Robinson, from the book *Shoeless Joe* by W.P. Kinsella. Photography: John Lindley. Design: Dennis Gassner. Editor: Ian Crafford. Music: James Horner.

Leading Players: Kevin Costner (Ray Kinsella), Amy

Madigan (Annie Kinsella), Gaby Hoffman (Karin Kinsella), Ray Liotta (Shoeless Joe Jackson), Timothy Busfield (Mark), James Earl Jones (Terence Mann), Burt Lancaster (Dr 'Moonlight' Graham), Frank Whaley (Archie Graham), Dwyer Brown (John Kinsella), Lee Garlington (Beulah).

REVENGE
Rastar/Columbia. 1990. 124 minutes.

Director: Tony Scott. Producers: Hunt Lowry, Stanley Rubin. Executive Producer: Kevin Costner. Screenplay: Jim Harrison, Jeffrey Fiskin, based on the novella by Jim Harrison. Photography: Jeffrey Kimball. Design: Michael Seymour, Benjamin Fernandez. Editor: Chris Lebenzon. Music: Jack Nitzsche.

Leading Players: Kevin Costner (Cochran), Anthony Quinn (Tiburon Mendez), Madeleine Stowe (Miryea), Tomas Milian (Cesar), Joaquin Martinez (Mauro), James Gammon (Texan), Jesse Corti (Madero), Sally Kirkland (Rock Star), Luis De Icaza (Ramon), Gerardo Zepeda (Elefante), Miguel Ferrer (Amador), John Leguizamo (Ignacio), Joe Santos (Ibarra), Christopher De Oni (Diaz), Karmin Murcelo (Madam).

DANCES WITH WOLVES
Tig Productions/Orion/Majestic. 1990. 179 minutes.

Director: Kevin Costner. Producers: Jim Wilson, Kevin Costner. Screenplay: Michael Blake. Photography: Dean Semler. Design: Jeffrey Beecroft. Editor: Neil Travis. Music: John Barry.

Leading Players: Kevin Costner (Lieutenant John J. Dunbar), Mary McDonnell (Stands with A Fist), Graham Greene (Kicking Bird), Rodney A. Grant (Wind In His Hair), Floyd Red Crow Westerman (Ten Bears), Tantoo Cardinal (Black Shawl), Jimmy Herman (Stone Calf), Charles Rocket (Lieutenant Elgin), Robert Pastorelli (Timmons), Larry Joshua (Sergeant Bauer), Tony Pierce (Spivey), Tom Everett (Sergeant Pepper), Maury Chaykin (Major Farnbrough).

ROBIN HOOD PRINCE OF THIEVES
Morgan Creek/Warner Bros. 1991. 141 minutes.

Director: Kevin Reynolds. Producers: John Watson, Pen Densham, Richard B. Lewis. Screenplay: Pen Densham, John Watson, from a story by Pen Densham. Photography: Douglas Milsome. Design: John Graysmark. Editor: Peter Boyle. Music: Michael Kamen.

Leading Players: Kevin Costner (Robin of Locksley), Morgan Freeman (Azeem), Christian Slater (Will Scarlett), Alan Rickman (Sheriff of Nottingham), Mary Elizabeth Mastrantonio (Marian), Geraldine McEwan (Mortianna), Michael McShane (Friar Tuck), Brian Blessed (Lord Locksley), Michael Wincott (Guy of Gisborne), Nick Brimble (John Little), Soo Drouet (Fanny), Daniel Newman (Wulf), Daniel Peacock (Bull), Walter Sparrow (Duncan), Harold Innocent (Bishop of Hereford).

IN BED WITH MADONNA
Dino De Laurentiis/Propaganda Films/Boy Toy. 1991. 119 minutes.

Director: Alek Keshishian. Producers: Jay Roewe, Tim Clawson. Photography: Robert Leacock, Doug Nichol, Toby Phillips. Editor: Barry Alexander Brown.

Leading Players: Madonna, Sandra Bernhard, Donna Delory, Niki Harris, Moira McFarland-Messana, Warren Beatty, Kevin Costner.

JFK
Warner Bros/Le Studio Canal Plus/Regency Enterprises/ Alcor Films. 1991. 189 minutes.

Director: Oliver Stone. Producers: A. Kitman Ho, Oliver Stone. Screenplay: Oliver Stone, Zachary Sklar, based on the books *On the Trail of the Assassins* by Jim Garrison and *Crossfire: the plot that killed Kennedy* by Jim Marrs. Photography: Robert Richardson. Design: Victor Kempster. Editors: Joe Hutshing, Pietro Scalia, Hank Corwin. Music: John Williams.

Leading Players: Kevin Costner (Jim Garrison), Gary Oldman (Lee Harvey Oswald), Sissy Spacek (Liz Garrison), Tommy Lee Jones (Clay Shaw), Kevin Bacon (Willie O'Keefe), Donald Sutherland (Colonel 'X'), John Candy (Dean Andrews), Joe Pesci (David Ferrie), Laurie Metcalf (Susie Cox), Michael Rooker (Bill Broussard), Jay O. Saunders (Lou Ivon), Sally Kirkland (Rose Cheramie), Anthony Ramirez (Epileptic), Ray LePere (Zapruder), Ed Asner (Guy Banister), Jack Lemmon (Jack Martin), Vincent D'Onofrio (Bill Newman), Steve Reed (John F. Kennedy Double), Jodi Farber (Jackie Kennedy Double), Columbia Dubose (Nellie Connally Double), Randy Means (Governor Connally Double), Walter Matthau (Senator Russell Long).

Index

Alexander, Jane, 47
Allen, Phillip R., 69
Allen, Woody, 16
Amazing Chuck and Grace, 96
Amazing Stories (see *The Mission*)
American Flyers, 55–9
Amos, John, 57
Ansen, David, 58
Armstrong, Gillian, 118
Arnaz, Desi, 82
Arquette, Rosanna, 62, 65
Atlantic City, 98, 109
Attenborough, Richard, 35
Autry, Gene, 145
Avellone, Greg, 24
Avildsen, John G., 55

Back to the Future II, 113
Bacon, Kevin, 167
Badham, John, 44, 55, 56, 58, 118
Bailey, John, 65
Baker, Ray, 62
Baldwin, Alec, 119
Ball, Lucille, 82
Bara, Theda, 42
Barrie, J.M., 114
Batman, 168
Battleship Potemkin, 77
Baxter, Warner, 145
The Beast, 117, 118
The Beast of War (see *The Beast*)
Beatty, Warren, 159
Beetlejuice, 156

Benedek, Barbara, 45
Bercovici, Luca, 57
Berenger, Tom, 44, 45, 118
Bergin, Patrick, 144, 149-150
Bergson, Philip, 64
Best of Times, The, 97
Betrayed, 118
Beverly Hills Cop II, 120
Big Chill, The, 16, 43-7, 55, 60, 118
Big Clock, The, 93
Blake, Michael, 30, 38, 41-2, 120, 127-9, 132, 133, 135, 138, 140
Blessed, Brian, 152
Blinko, Philip, 13
Bloomfield, John, 147
Blow Out, 70
Bodyguard, The, 170
Body Heat, 45
Bogdanovitch, Peter, 118
Born on the Fourth of July, 163
Botsford, Sara, 48
Bounty, The, 88
Bowie, David, 120
Boyle, Peter, 151
Brander, Leslie, 29
Brander, Richard, 29
Branstad, Terry, 115
Breaking Away, 55, 56
Brewster's Millions, 96
Bridges, Jeff, 118
Brimble, Nick, 153
Brode, Douglas, 115
Broken Arrow, 133

Brooks, Mel, 16
Broughton, Bruce, 65
Brown, David G., 32
Brown, Dee, 128
Brown, Dwyer, 112
Brown, Geoff, 79
Bull Durham, 17, 55, 97-104, 105, 109, 129
Bunyan, Paul, 19
Burne, Jerome, 46
Burton, Richard, 25, 80, 140
Burton, Sir Richard, 144
Bury my Heart at Wounded Knee (book), 128
Busfield, Timothy, 111
Bush, Chuck, 50
Bush, George, 164-5

Cage, Nicholas, 118
Caine, Michael, 70
Camelot, 170
Canby, Vincent, 156
Capone, Al, 68-77, 79, 80
Capra, Frank, 15, 106, 113, 114
Carrie, 70
Castillo, Nardo, 47
Cesak, Brian, 50
Chandler, Jeff, 133
Charge, Doris Leader, 133
Chasing Dreams, 32–3, 44, 55, 97
Chaykin, Maury, 135
Cher, 118
Chong, Rae Dawn, 57
Cimino, Michael, 60, 129, 131
Cleese, John, 62, 65
Clifford, Graeme, 35, 36
Close, Glenn, 44, 46
Coen, Joel, 118
Collinson, Peter, 125
Come and Get It, 34
Compton, G.D., 20
Compton-Burnett, Ivy, 103
Congie, Terry, 31
Connery, Jason, 145
Connery, Sean, 68, 69, 73, 78, 79, 80, 94, 119, 145, 149, 150, 155
Cooper, Gary, 13, 15, 16, 95, 106, 114, 128, 170, 171
Corliss, Richard, 64

Corti, Jesse, 122
Costner, Annie, 81
Costner, Dan, 20, 22, 135
Costner, Joe, 81
Costner, Lily, 81
Costner, Sharon, 20, 24, 25, 134
Costner, William, 19–21, 24, 25, 134
Count of Monte Cristo, The, 152
Coward, Noël, 104
Crenna, Richard, 43
Crossfire (book), 166
Cruise, Tom, 120
Custer, General, 19

Dafoe, William, 118
Damn Yankees, 96
Dances with Wolves, 17, 38, 49, 66, 78, 87, 126, 127-141, 143, 146, 151, 154, 156, 158, 159, 164, 165, 168, 169, 171
Darling, Ron, 115
Daves, Delmer, 133
Day After, The, 47
De Icaza, Luis, 123
De Lillo, Don, 164
De Niro, Robert, 13, 14, 68–9, 72, 78–9, 80, 94, 141
De Palma, Brian, 68–71, 77, 84
Dean, James, 51
Demme, Jonathan, 109
Dempster, Nigel, 158
Dennehy, Brian, 62
Densham, Pen, 143
Dickinson, Angie, 70
Die Hard, 147, 156
Disney, Walt, 20, 24, 146
Donaldson, Roger, 88, 93
Drago, Billy, 73
Dressed to Kill, 70
Driving Miss Daisy, 147
Dzundza, George, 90

Eastwood, Clint, 61, 88
Ebert, Roger, 58, 80, 99
Edwards, Anthony, 120
Ehrenstein, David, 117
Eight Men Out, 96
Eisenstein, Sergei, 77

Elliott, Sam, 118
Engelson, George J., 31
Errigo, Angie, 141
Eszterhas, Joe, 118
Everybody's All-American, 96, 118

Fairbanks, Douglas, 145, 154
Fandango, 17, 23, 37, 38, 49–55, 64, 66, 87, 117, 118, 134, 143, 146, 164
Farmer, Frances, 34–6
Fearing, Kenneth, 87
Ferrer, Miguel, 123
Ferrie, David, 167
Field of Dreams, 17, 55, 78, 97, 105–16, 120, 154
Floyd, Nigel, 126
Flynn, Errol, 142, 145, 154
Fonda, Henry, 36
Forbes, Bryan, 35
Ford, Gerald, 164
Ford, Harrison, 68, 88
Ford, John, 21
Fox, Edward, 150
Frances, 34–6, 44
Freeman, Morgan, 66, 147, 152
Fuesel, Bob, 69
Fuller, David, 141
Funny Girl, 25

Gable, Clark, 99
Gammon, James, 123, 124
Gance, Abel, 141
Garcia, Andy, 73
Garland, Robert, 87, 93
Garlington, Lee, 111
Garrison, Jim, 162, 164, 166, 168, 169
Gehring, Lou, 95
Ghost, 155
Giant, 51
Gibson, Mel, 15, 68, 88, 118, 143
Glengarry, Glen Ross (play), 71
Glenn, Scott, 61, 64
Glover, Danny, 61, 62, 66
Go to the Head of the Class, 85
Goldblum, Jeff, 44, 46, 63
Goldwyn, Sam, 95
Gone with the Wind, 99

Goodrich, Frances, 113
Gordon, Charles, 107
Gordon, Lawrence, 107, 115
Grant, Cary, 148
Grant, David, 56, 58
Grant, Rodney A., 132
Greene, Graham, 132
Greene, Richard, 145, 146
Grey, Jennifer, 89
Gunrunner, The, 16, 30, 32, 47–8

Hackett, Albert, 113
Hackman, Gene, 87, 89, 93
Halliwell, Leslie, 46
Hardy, Phil, 126
Harris, J.J., 54, 108, 158
Harris, Richard, 133
Harrison, Jim, 119
Hathaway, Henry, 21
Hawks, Howard, 34, 70
Heaven's Gate, 60, 129, 131
Hepburn, Audrey, 145
Herbert, A.P., 169
Hi, Mom!, 70
High Noon, 63
Hitler, Adolf, 163
Hoffman, Dustin, 41
Hoffman, Gaby, 108, 110
Homicide, 71
Hook, 114
Hopkins, Anthony, 88
Hoskins, Bob, 69
Houck, Roy, 134
House of Games, 71
Houston, Whitney, 170
How the West Was Won, 13, 21, 67
Howard, Ron, 37
Howarth, Garth, 40
Hughes, John, 108
Hunger, The, 120
Hunt for Red October, The, 119
Hunt, Linda, 63, 65, 135
Hurt, William, 44, 45, 46, 68
Huston, Danny, 120
Huston, John, 119–20, 121, 126
Huston, Tony, 119

In Bed with Madonna, 159
In the Mood, 106

Index

Innocent, Harold, 153, 155
Irons, Jeremy, 140
Irvin, John, 149
It's a Wonderful Life, 113

Jackson, (Shoeless) Joe, 96, 109, 110–12, 114, 115, 116
Jagged Edge, 118
James, Bill, 115
Jenkins, Jane, 34
JFK, 16, 17, 18, 78, 87, 92, 104, 163–9, 171
Joffe, Roland, 118
Johnston, Sheila, 43
Johnstone, Iain, 168
Jones, James Earl, 108, 111, 113
Jones, Shirley, 25
Jones, Tommy Lee, 167

Kael, Pauline, 15, 63, 80, 91, 114, 139, 163, 165
Kasdan, Lawrence, 33, 43–5, 49, 60–2, 64–5, 68, 135
Kasdan, Mark, 61
Keaton, Michael, 37
Kelly, Gene, 95
Kennedy, Jacqueline, 167
Kennedy, John F., 131, 161–7, 169
Keshishian, Alek, 159
Killing Fields, The, 118
King, Martin Luther, 167
Kinsella, W.P., 107
Kirkland, Sally, 123, 124
Kline, Kevin, 61, 64
Korngold, Erich Wolfgang, 154
Krays, The, 125
Kulzer, William J., 31, 32

Lady in Red, The, 69
Lancaster, Burt, 109, 112
Lanchester, Elsa, 93
Lange, Jessica, 35
Latimer, Jonathan, 93
Laughton, Charles, 87, 93
Lawrence of Arabia, 141
Lean, David, 141, 148
Lerner, Alan Jay, 170
Lethal Weapon, 68
Lieberman, Robert, 43

Lilith, Eve, 38, 41, 42
Linson, Art, 69, 72
Liotta, Ray, 109, 111
Lippet, Barbara, 139
Littman, Lynne, 47
Loewe, Frederick, 170
Louzil, Eric, 28
Lowe, Rob, 13
Lust for Life, 121

McDonnell, Mary, 132, 138
McEwan, Geraldine, 147, 153, 155
McIntyre, Marvin J., 52
MacLaine, Shirley, 139
McQueen, Steve, 69, 88, 171
Madigan, Amy, 108, 110
Madison, Guy, 60
Madonna, 33, 118, 159
Malamud, Bernard, 96
Malibu Hot Summer (see *Sizzle Beach*)
Mamet, David, 69, 70, 71, 74, 75, 76, 77, 80
Man Called Horse, A, 133
Mankiewicz, Herman, 95
Marrs, Jim, 166
Marshall, George, 21
Martinez, Joaquin, 123
Mary Poppins, 148
Mary Rose, 114
Mask, 118
Mastrantonio, Mary Elizabeth, 147, 152
Maugham, Somerset, 84
Medak, Peter, 125
Mehta, Zubin, 34
Men of Sherwood Forest, 146
Meyjes, Menno, 84
Miami Vice, 64
Mike's Murder, 33, 43, 118
Milian, Tomas, 122
Milland, Ray, 87
Millian, Andra, 38, 41
Mission, The, 84–7
Mississippi Burning, 118
Monroe, Marilyn, 167
Mount, Thorn, 103
Mountains of the Moon, 144
Mr North, 120

Mr Smith Goes to Washington, 168
Mrs Soffel, 118
Mummy Daddy, 85
Muni, Paul, 70
Murder a la Mod, 70
Murphy, Eddie, 120

Napoleon, 141
Natten, Markus, 85
Natural, The, 96
Nelson, Judd, 50
Ness, Eliot, 68–80, 166, 169
Newman, Kim, 85
Newman, Paul, 36, 71
Nicita, Wally, 33, 43
Night Shift, 37, 44
No Place to Hide, 32
No Way Out, 87–94, 95, 105, 129
None But the Lonely Heart, 148
North, Oliver, 92

Odets, Clifford, 34
Oklahoma!, 53
O'Leary, William, 102
On the Trail of the Assassins (book), 162
O'Sullivan, Maureen, 87
Oswald (book), 164
Oswald, Lee Harvey, 101, 104, 161–2, 166
Ovitz, Mike, 108, 158

Pacino, Al, 14
Pale Rider, 61
Parker, Alan, 118
Parton, Dolly, 106
Pastorelli, Robert, 135
Patkin, Will, 99
Patton, Will, 89, 93
Paul, Alexandra, 57
Peary, Danny, 46
Perry, George, 156
Pesci, Joe, 167
Peter Pan, 114
Place, Mary Kay, 46
Platoon, 118, 163
Player to be Named Later, A (play), 97

Pleskow, Eric, 66
Pollock, Tom, 16
Praed, Michael, 145
Price, Frank, 99
Pride of the Yankees, The, 95
Priestley, J.B., 114
Profumo, John, 92
Proof, 49
Pryor, Richard, 96
Puttnam, David, 117, 119
Pygmalion, 106

Quaid, Dennis, 96
Quinn, Anthony, 119, 121, 124

Rabid Grannies, 28
Raging Bull, 78
Raiders of the Lost Ark, 147
Raising Arizona, 118
Redford, Robert, 88, 96, 141
Return of the Jedi, 108
Return of the Secaucus Seven, 45
Revenge, 15, 38, 105, 119–26, 179
Reversal of Fortune, 140
Reynolds, Kevin, 14, 49, 54, 117, 134, 143–52, 154–6
Reynolds, Mike, 38
Rhinestone, 106
Rickman, Alan, 147, 151, 152, 154
Robards, Sam, 50
Robbins, Tim, 99, 100
Roberts, Julia, 144
Robertson, Jenny, 100
Robin and Marian, 145
Robin and the Seven Hoods, 145
Robin Hood (Bergin), 144, 149–50
Robin Hood (Flynn), 142
Robin Hood of El Dorado, 145
Robin Hood: Prince of Thieves, 54, 66, 142–9, 151–6, 160, 164, 165, 171
Robinson, David, 80
Robinson, James, 143, 148, 155
Robinson, Phil Alden, 105–7, 113–6, 120
Rocky, 55
Rocky Horror Show, The, 98
Room with a View, A, 153
Rose Tattoo, The, 109

Ruby, Jack, 162
Rule, Janice, 56, 58
Rumpelstiltskin (play), 24

Salvador, 163
Sarandon, Susan, 82, 98, 100, 103, 109
Sayles, John, 96
Scarface, 70
Schickel, Richard, 139
Schwarzenegger, Arnold, 15, 106, 115
Scott, Tony, 120, 125, 126
Seance on a Wet Afternoon, 35
Semler, Dean, 138
Shadows Run Black, 30–2, 44
Shanghai Surprise, 118
Shaw, Clay, 162, 166, 167
Sheenan, Henry, 168
Shelton, Ron, 97–98, 100, 103
Shoeless Joe (see *Field of Dreams*)
Shoeless Joe (novel), 107
Shoes of the Fisherman, The, 121
Siemaszko, Casey, 85
Silva, Cindy, 24–7, 29–30, 80–3, 134, 135, 140, 157–8, 164, 170
Silverado, 17, 45, 60–7, 69, 87, 128, 129, 134, 135, 138, 164
Simkin, Margery, 47
Simon, John, 91
Simon, Paul, 115
Sinatra, Frank, 95, 145
Sizzle Beach, 24, 28–9, 32, 44, 89
Sizzle Beach USA (see *Sizzle Beach*)
Slater, Christian, 147, 153, 155
Sleeping with the Enemy, 144
Smith, Charles Martin, 73
Snow, Mat, 126
Something Wild, 109
Son of Fury, 34
Spacek, Sissy, 166
Sparrow, Walter, 152
Spielberg, Steven, 49, 68, 84, 114, 151
Spottiswoode, Roger, 97
Stack, Robert, 69
Stacy's Knights, 30, 38–43, 44, 127, 130

Stallone, Sylvester, 15, 32, 55, 106
Stanley, Kim, 35
Star Wars, 108
Stark, Ray, 119–120
Stewart, James, 13, 15, 16, 21, 67, 72, 106, 113, 114, 128, 133, 168, 170, 171
Stewart, Sheri, 157–8
Stone, Oliver, 118, 161, 163–9
Story of Robin Hood and his Merrie Men, The, 146
Stowe, Madeleine, 121, 124
Strada, La, 121
Streisand, Barbra, 140
Stroheim, Erich Von, 60
Surf Nazis Must Die, 28
Sutherland, Kiefer, 85
Swayze, Patrick, 89
Swerling, Joe, 95
Sword of Sherwood Forest, 146

Table for Five, 43, 44
Take Me Out to the Ball Game, 95
Taylor, Don, 146
Tesich, Steve, 55–6, 58–9
Testament, 47
Things Change, 71
Thomas, Philip, 156
Thurman, Uma, 150
Tierney, Gene, 34
Todd, Richard, 146
Top Gun, 120
Travolta, John, 70
Trosper, Elziabeth, 31
Truth or Dare (see *In Bed with Madonna*)
Turner, Kathleen, 45

Under Fire, 97
Untouchables, The (film), 17, 21, 68–80, 87, 91, 93, 95, 154, 164, 166
Untouchables, The (TV series), 69

Van Damme, Jean-Claude, 15
Van Dyke, Dick, 148
Velasco, Irma, 54
Verdict, The, 71

Viva Zapata, 121
Voight, Jon, 43

Wall Street, 163
WarGames, 44, 55, 118
Warner, Jack, 142
Warren, Earl, 162
Watson, John, 143, 148
Wayne, John, 60, 128, 139
Weisburg, Harold, 163
Welles, Orson, 139
Wells, Dominic, 84
Westerman, Floyd Red Crow, 136
Whaley, Frank, 112
Whitfield, Lynn, 63
Whitman, Walt, 101, 102
Wilde, Cornel, 166
Williams, Esther, 95
Williams, John, 86
Willis, Bruce, 15
Wilson, James, 30, 38, 42, 130, 132, 168

Wincott, Michael, 153, 155
Winkler, Henry, 37
Winning Streak (see *Stacy's Knights*)
Wisecarver, Sonny (Woo Woo), 106–7
Wizard of Oz, The, 114
Wolff, Al, 69
Wolfit, Donald, 108
Woo Woo Kid, The (see *In the Mood*),
Wood, Sam, 95
Wright, Robin, 147
Wyler, William, 34

Yates, Peter, 55
Young, Sean, 82, 87, 89, 92–3

Ziskin, Laura, 88, 96
Zorba the Greek, 121